Department of Agriculture

Modern Dairying

Department of Agriculture

Modern Dairying

ISBN/EAN: 9783743337299

Manufactured in Europe, USA, Canada, Australia, Japa

Cover: Foto ©Andreas Hilbeck / pixelio.de

Manufactured and distributed by brebook publishing software
(www.brebook.com)

Department of Agriculture

Modern Dairying

DEPARTMENT OF AGRICULTURE, VICTORIA,

MODERN DAIRYING,

BY

MESSRS. D. WILSON AND R. CROWE,

DAIRY EXPERTS.

𝕭𝔂 𝖅𝖚𝖙𝖍𝖔𝖗𝖎𝖙𝖞:

ROBT. S, BRAIN, GOVERNMENT PRINTER, MELBOURNE.

1898.

3063

PREFACE.

In no other industry has there been more rapid changes in recent years than in that of Dairying.

The machinery and utensils invented a few years ago are being greatly improved, and many are now quite out of date. Inventive minds are constantly at work to improve existing methods.

Chemists, bacteriologists, and others skilled in science have given earnest attention to investigating and improving the properties of dairy products.

The necessity has therefore arisen for the publication of an up-to-date manual for the information of those engaged in Victoria in the Dairying Industry. The production of such a work, while being of special interest to the advanced butter and cheese maker, will also, it is hoped, prove of service to all milk suppliers and dairy produce manufacturers.

The two dairy experts—Messrs. D. Wilson and R. Crowe—attached to this Department have devoted themselves to the task of producing a work which, I trust, will be found to give all the information which correspondents with the Department are frequently asking for.

The advice tendered, it is hoped, will have the effect of causing improvement on the part of some suppliers and manufacturers, for no matter how advanced a country may be in its methods of producing, there are always some laggards who bring reproach on those whose desires are to advance and not retard. We live in a progressive age. Times change, and we must change with them if we are to prosper.

The marvellous progress which has taken place in the Dairying Industry in Victoria is almost a matter of history, and came as a surprise to other countries ; and, aided as we are by science, the extent of its further development and expansion is almost incomprehensible. It therefore behoves us to exercise the greatest care in keeping up and increasing the high standard we have reached. It is the ambition of the Department to keep in the front of all the British possessions as regards the industry to which this *brochure* has reference, and it is sincerely hoped that the object desired may be accomplished somewhat by the information herein contained.

D. MARTIN,
Secretary for Agriculture.

Department of Agriculture,
Melbourne, April, 1898.

MODERN DAIRYING.

FACTORY BUTTER-MAKING.

Rules for butter-making could easily be drawn up if the conditions under which each butter-maker laboured were alike. If the milk were in the same order, the climatic conditions identical, and like appliances used, it could readily be disposed of. The conditions in different localities and places vary. The circumstances are also constantly changing in each place. It would be of little advantage, therefore, to frame rules without pointing out a method of applying them. More good will be derived from a general discussion of the subject. The subject will be shown from different stand-points, and it is hoped that in such form it will prove of the best service.

The quality of butter largely depends on the treatment of the milk before it reaches the factory or creamery, and the condition of the milk when it reaches the butter-maker's hands.

THE CARE OF MILK.

Milk should be drawn from the cows in as cleanly a manner as possible. The surroundings should also receive due attention.

It is a pleasure to notice the recent rapid increase of modern well-drained and paved milking-yards; together with well-arranged and ventilated milking-sheds.

Examples can be met with in every district that serve as models for the neighbours to copy. When yards are convenient in their arrangement and paved it is easy and pleasant to work in and keep them clean.

Milk is a great absorbent of bad odours, and a good medium for the development of bacteria. If the surroundings be evil-smelling the milk will soon become tainted. The value of butter, therefore, becomes lessened as the contamination is permitted to increase in the milk.

If a cow's udder is dirty it should be carefully washed, and if clean it should at least be wiped. Such simple precautions prevent filth and dust from falling into the bucket when milking. Milking with dry hands is preferable, and is fast coming into favour. It is a much cleaner and better plan than the old way.

Milk should be kept in a clean place shaded from the rays of the sun, and away from dust and smells.

The milk vessels and everything that the milk comes in contact with should be absolutely clean. The temperature of the milk should be reduced as rapidly as possible after it comes from the cow. (See Rules for Milk and Cream Supply, page 32.)

'When the milk is strong in odour and flavour from such food as fresh green rape, lucerne, trefoil, turnips, &c., aeration greatly improves it.

The aeration of milk has long been advocated; but because it was imperfectly understood, or entailed a certain amount of trouble, but few dairymen practise it. Milk that is quite nauseous to the taste, and gives off a strong undesirable odour from the above causes, can be made quite agreeable and palatable by aerating. The fact that the odour rises from the milk is proof that the element causing it is volatile. If pure air is passed through the milk, or if milk is spread out thinly and exposed to such air, the undesirable element evaporates and is carried away. A simple experiment may be more convincing than any lengthy explanation. When the milk is affected take a cupful and pour it a few times from one cup into another. In doing so let the milk fall some distance through the air. After this is done a great improvement will be noticed. The same thing may be done by means of dippers or buckets; but when large quantities are handled special appliances have been designed—and are in the market—for effecting the object. The process is greatly assisted if carried out when the milk is at a high temperature immediately after coming from the cow.

Recent experiments have been made to find out if it were possible to eliminate this injurious element at the creamery instead of the farm. Considerable success was met with, and the matter is dealt with elsewhere under the head of "Pasteurizing."

Farmers reason in the following manner:—"My milk is considered good enough to be taken at the creamery without my going to any bother with it, and anything that is considered good enough to receive there is quite good enough to send."

Again:—"If I put my milk in the best condition, and make it most suitable for manufacturing a tip-top quality of butter, and my neighbour does not, my good work is negatived by his carelessness as soon as our milk is mixed at the creamery. He gets as much for his product as I do who supply a superior article."

This contention applies to all milk inferior in condition, as well as from the neglect of proper aeration when necessary. This is really the weakest point in our otherwise excellent co-operative system of dairying.

It has often been suggested that the remedy rests with the companies; that they should extend the system of payment by results, and pay for the milk according to the condition as well as according to the butter contained.

Many difficulties present themselves in the carrying out of such a proposal. The chief obstacle is the want of a definite measure of the suitability of milk for butter-making at the time of its delivery at the factory. The determination of respective values would have to be placed entirely in the hands of the manager, and applied at his discretion.

As his employers are generally suppliers and are often offenders, undesirable friction would sometimes be caused if the manager did his duty. Of course the same argument was put forward when the system of payment according to butter contents was initiated, but the cases differ considerably. In the one instance there is great definiteness in the result, which can be checked if a doubt arises. In the other no such precision exists. It was at one time suggested as practicable, in cases of dispute, to have the question settled by a board of reference from the suppliers present at the moment. Such a course would in many cases—if not all—take the responsibility off the manager's shoulders, but could not give ultimate satisfaction. The sole power of exercising judgment should be vested in the manager's hands.

Authority is given at present in nearly all places for the manager to refuse to take delivery of milk unfit for the making of good butter, but the line in 90 per cent. of our factories is drawn too low.

If milk will pass through the separator it is generally considered good enough to take, and sourness, or the degree of sourness, is the only point taken into account in some places in determining the suitability of the milk.

Very often milk which is too sour for separating is better suited for making a good butter than another class of milk which has been tainted through having been kept in unclean surroundings, or in dirty vessels. This is the class of milk that causes most damage in the factory. It often arrives sweet to the taste, but having a bad odour.

Such milk is responsible for far more trouble and deterioration in the finished product than milk that has naturally soured through being kept at too high a temperature. It is that class of milk that presents the greatest difficulties in determining its value.

There is another phase of the subject, and one that presents as practical a solution of the difficulty as is likely to be found. In our best managed factories the milk is generally all good. The reason is that the manager exercises a wise influence over the producers.

If milk is brought that is not up to the mark, the fault is pointed out, and advice given how to remedy it. Should the cause be of such a nature as to render it easily overcome, no excuse is taken after the first warning, and the delivery of such milk is promptly refused. If the remedy is difficult to apply, more latitude is given, advice and help are tendered, and the same firmness is displayed in dealing with the supplier. It is in such firm supervision of the milk supply where most of our factories score and succeed. It is in the want of such safeguard, and, necessarily, sure foundation, that so many fail to make good butter. A good builder makes a secure foundation before he erects a structure that he wishes to last long and reflect credit on him. So a good manager or butter-maker has to take similar precautions. Managers should have full control in all matters pertaining to the quality of the butter. The exercise of such authority always demands the greatest tact. It would be an easy matter to make one's methods of dealing objectionable, and drive the suppliers away. Great changes for the better should be brought about gradually in a factory.

Suppliers should recognise that their factory manager has to daily act as an arbitrator in matters relating to their welfare. First of all there is the relationship between the shareholders of the company and the milk suppliers to be borne in mind. Then there is fair play to be meted out between one supplier and another. And the manager has to protect his reputation by turning out a good article. It is a delicate position to fill well. In a few instances where full control is given the necessary backbone is wanting, proper authority is not exercised, and the energies of the manager are sometimes misdirected, undue attention being paid to certain branches of his work.

The manager, in some cases, is always to be found behind the butter-worker, concentrating his main efforts to the make, the build, the texture, and finish of his butter. Such points are all necessary, and should receive their due share of attention. But what is the good of a butter perfectly made and got up if it is wanting in bouquet and flavour?

Flavour is the great essential in good butter. All the other points—texture, salting, packing, colour, &c.—embrace the condition of the butter, and can be easily controlled and regulated. The great desideratum is flavour. It is the fineness of flavour that makes butter sell at a shilling a pound, and it is the want of it that causes an equally good butter in other respects to bring only eightpence in the same market. Any manager, therefore, who does not make the flavour his chief study and object is not working in the best direction.

The greatest success attends those who make the condition in which the raw material, the milk or cream, reaches their hands their first care. It does not follow that they must always be present when the milk is being received. Instructions to those who take the milk should be definite and pointed, and in large places an occasional visit to see that it is done properly is generally sufficient. Suppliers should not think that any hardships are proposed to be laid upon them. The proportion of careless suppliers that really require looking after is small, and it is not fair that for the faults of those few the quality of the produce belonging to the great majority should be lowered.

We have attained uniformity in individual factories, but in many the standard is too low, owing principally to want of strictness in looking after the milk supply. Without a standard of excellence in his mind the butter-maker cannot tell what he is aiming for. Each has an idea of what a perfect butter should be, the same as every one has a different standard for cleanliness. What one considers perfect another often thinks far from perfect.

A butter-maker who aims at making the kind of butter that the customers like the best, and are prepared to pay most money for, cannot go far wrong. Never mind catering for individual fancy, not even your own. If your butter is to be consumed in Melbourne, make it to suit Melbourne customers. If for West Australia or Cape Colony, make and prepare it in the manner and shape preferred there ; and if for London, try and study the best means of manufacture that will cause it to give best satisfaction there. The hard matter in connexion with this is to secure reliable reports as to how the butter suits the consumers.

The account sales serve as the best indicator ; but very often a 112s. report accompanies a 105s. price. It is considered business to take steps to secure the continuance of butter through one's hands, no matter what the quality of it is. The opinion of the consumer, if not flattering, must therefore be withheld, or trimmed into such shape so as not to run the risk of losing that brand another season. Producers are often naturally suspicious that a report drawing attention to faults is framed to justify low prices.

This is a delicate and important point, that may eventually call for a more satisfactory method of dealing with that would be more agreeable and satisfactory to all parties.

Too many of our butter-makers miss this great point altogether. They strive to make an article that pleases themselves—an article which, at the time of manufacture, is good and nice.

They do not follow it up, and try to find out how it stood the journey to the consumer, and what effect the variations in temperature had on it. Rarely do they closely inquire as to how it stood the tests of the buyers, and suited the consumers.

From this it will be seen what an important part the care of the milk takes in making good butter. It is little use to expect to make choicest butter from milk any proportion of which is not good. However, the question has to be faced as it is, not as it ought to be. In many localities it is more than a man's position is worth to refuse milk and cream not first class.

The following extract from a factory manager's letter will serve to illustrate how matters stand :—

I am not at all surprised to hear you complain about our output being bad in flavour. I am far from satisfied with the general quality of our export make ; but I can assure you that I have done my level best with the material I am obliged to handle.

Eighty per cent. of our business is hand or turbine separator trade, and during the summer months I find it is impossible to make anything like a first-class article.

Some of the suppliers are far from being clean, whilst others keep the cream too long on hand, and give it no attention. A few of my suppliers are very careful people, whose cream always reaches me in the best of condition, but the majority are hard to do business with.

· The small separators are rapidly increasing, and are accountable for so much bad cream. They have come to stay in some districts, so I think it is time something was done to protect the export trade. I cannot remedy the evil at the factory, neither do I think any man can do so. The cream is gone too far for that ere it reaches us. I have been amongst my suppliers, giving them any useful hints I knew of.

The results were an improvement for a few days, but they soon fell back to their old groove again. If I reject their cream some one else will take it, so I have to try and hold all kinds, good, bad, and indifferent. I think the Government should take some steps, and enforce stringent measures to rectify the matter.

I regret to say that most of the suppliers are indifferent, and do not care what harm they do, as long as they can get rid of the cream.

Eventually (if not protected) I am afraid the whole industry will suffer through this means. It is no use in waiting for any one else to make a move, and I don't think any other person's protest will carry so much weight as yours. I stand on delicate ground, and dare not take up the cudgels against my own suppliers, and so I am in hopes you will take some measures to cope with this evil before our next export season commences.

We are sorry to say that the above letter presents an exact statement of the position of affairs in a few cases. It is not general as yet, but is growing, and has a strong tendency to spread. To put it plainly, much harm has already been done to our export trade through the breaking down of the original co-operative system in some localities. A little further on and it will mean the forfeiture of our position in the world's markets, and not unlikely the wrecking of our export trade. To those not in the business a short explanation may not be out of place. The origina. splendid co-operative system was started on the following sound lines:—Factories and creameries were established where the milk was delivered by the farmers. The lots of cream were large enough then to warrant proper attention and prompt delivery to the factory, and the making of a uniform quality of butter of a high standard.

With our high-class butter of uniform quality we got a footing on the London market, and year by year gradually improved our position. Of recent years there has been a growing disposition on the part of dairymen to purchase small plants and separate their own milk ; the individual supply of cream is, consequently, so small that it is not worth special attention, and as the cream is only sent to the factory when convenient—three times a week, and often only once a week—it can be imagined that in our hot climate it frequently reaches the factory in an unsatisfactory condition. The foundation of our past success—uniformity—is thus being destroyed. The average quality is lowered in standard, and the cost of production and marketing increased. It is difficult to understand why dairymen are doing this with their eyes open. The danger is pointed out to them on every possible occasion. ' Of course, there is no alternative open to those who are not within reach of a creamery or factory, and they cannot be blamed. If the factory were to send round collectors daily it would add to the cost of production considerably, and it would also be undesirable to have inspectors who would insist on all cream being properly handled and cared for. Neither would it do, when butter from such cream is not best quality, to refuse its shipment, so the simplest way out of the difficulty would be to discard the system and dispose of the small machines to our opponents in other countries.

It is to be hoped that sufficient has been said to impress upon dairy farmers and dairy students the important part that the dairyman takes in the production of good butter. Having recognised that point we can now proceed to discuss the part allotted to the butter-maker.

SKIMMING.

A temperature of 80 deg. Fahr. is laid down as the most suitable temperature for skimming. At that temperature the cream is taken off cleaner and more readily than at a lower one. Good work can be done at a much lower temperature than 80 deg., but to do so the milk must be passed through the machine more slowly. There is a danger of the cream clogging when skimming at a low temperature. It is often necessary to skim at as low as 65 deg. in the summer months where there is insufficient refrigerating power available. It has been maintained that, if the temperature of the cream is over 80 deg. when skimming, the butter would be greasy. The texture of the butter is not, however, affected if the skimming be done at 160deg. The higher the temperature of the milk the more perfect the skimming, and the greater the quantity that may be passed through the separator with as good results.

The same thing holds good in regard to the speed of separators. The higher the rate of speed the better the separation, and more can be passed through with good results. The lower the speed the more imperfect the skimming, or to a certain point as good, but less work can be done. Separators should on no account be run much beyond their stated speed.

The essential points in good skimming are even temperature, even speed, and even feed.

Separators should be checked daily in their work. If samples be taken in a factory where a number of machines are working— all of the same make and estimated capacity, all being fed through the one pipe with milk of the same temperature, all driven by the same shaft, and going at the same rate of speed—and tested, it will be found that the results vary. In the skim-milk from No. 1 we will probably find 0·2 per cent. of butter fat; in that from No. 2, 0·025; from No. 3, 0·1; No. 4, 0·14; No. 5, 0·05, and so on.

This will not be found in a factory where the result is constantly tested and the machines properly adjusted. Machines are liable to go out of best form from time to time. In early separating days an average loss of under 0·15 per cent. of fat in the skim-milk was considered good, whilst at the present time any average loss of over 0·05 is considered bad skimming. Thus 0·1 per cent. of loss in a company's average turnover of 2,000 gallons a day, means in twelve months about 8,322 lbs. of butter not recovered. It will thus be seen that it pays to keep a sharp watch over the separators.

TREATMENT OF CREAM.

After the cream comes from the separator it should be cooled. The exact degree of cooling depends on the ripeness of the milk when skimming, the state of the weather, and when it is intended to be churned. When the milk has been separated in good condition, 65 deg. would be cool enough temperature for the cream, as the cream will ripen more rapidly than at a lower temperature. If the milk was ripe at the time of separating, the cream should be cooled to 60 deg., or according to the degree of ripeness. Should the weather be warm and close the lower the cream will have to be reduced in temperature to retard ripening, and if the day is cold the higher the cream may be left in temperature to hasten the ripening. When the churning is to be done on the day following separating, the more rapid must the ripening be made, and slower when the cream is left till two days old. The cream can be hastened in ripening by the addition of a starter, such as good buttermilk, or a culture prepared in skim or new milk. (Cultures are dealt with elsewhere under the head of "Pasteurizing.") Churning has to be done as soon as practicable after separating, but not before a certain degree of lactic acidity has been developed.

In many factories it is practicable to churn on the day following separating, whilst in many others it is not convenient to do so till two days afterwards. In all well-regulated places there is a time-table arranged and followed as closely as possible.

The cream is prepared so as to be right for churning when churning hour arrives. Authorities differ widely as to how cream should be treated from the time of separating till the time of churning. Managers have been met with who, after separating, cooled the cream down to 64 deg., and gradually to 58 deg., and churned it on the following morning. By this treatment butter was made that brought highest prices for each consignment right through the season in England. Again, another factory manager cooled the cream to 67 deg. or 68 deg., left it at that temperature for 24 hours, then cooling to 54 deg., and after another 24 hours, churning and making a butter that brought equally high prices. Both systems had been adopted as the result of many years' close practical study of the business. The goal is secured in different places by sometimes widely differing routes, and it would be invidious to say that either way was wrong.

At many places sufficient refrigerating power is not available to enable the manager to control the temperature as he would wish. It is when placed in such a position that the resourceful man comes out on top. A great deal can be done in some places without a refrigerator.

If plenty of cold water is at hand the cans of cream may be put into the water. After a time the water becomes warm with the heat abstracted from the cream and should then be replaced. Mistakes are often made by leaving the cans in the water when the atmosphere is colder.

Placing wet bags round the cans when neither cold air or water is procurable is a good plan.

At any place where much butter is made the aid of a refrigerator is imperative in the summer months. A man's surroundings or environments will always suggest methods of treatment for the cream.

TESTING ACIDITY OF CREAM.

During the last two seasons many systems have been adopted at our factories for recording the acidity of cream before churning. It is unfortunate that one standard system was not carried out. At many places alkaline tablets are used. Some use acidimetric tablets. Others use phenolphthalein as an indicator, and an alkali —either lime water, caustic soda, or potash solution—to determine the percentage of lactic acid. Again, a difference is found in the method of applying the various tests. One adds the solution to pure cream, another to a 50 per cent. cream solution, and the next to a $33\frac{1}{3}$ per cent. solution.

The data recorded is of the greatest value to the buttermakers themselves, but difficulties are met with when an attempt is made to compare experiences. Working from so many standpoints is prejudicial to mutual improvement—the policy of the Australasian Butter and Cheese Factories Managers' Association. It would assist the progress of the industry if that body were to discuss this matter and agree to the adoption of a uniform system as a standard. Doubtless a comparison could be made by finding the percentage of lactic acid per the respective systems. Hitherto this was impracticable, as the rules available failed to give corresponding results, either the tablets or the tables being incorrect. About 0·6 per cent. of lactic acid is the quantity required to be developed in cream before churning. The percentage should range from 0·55 to 0·65 per cent. of acid.

The system that gives best satisfaction is known as the Titration method. This test is based on the fact that if an alkaline solution is added to an acid solution a point is reached where the mixture is neither acid nor alkaline. Then, if an alkali of known strength is used, all that remains necessary is an indicator by which to tell when the point of neutrality is reached.

The apparatus required for the test is a 20 c.c. burette for measuring the cream, a 50 c.c. glass-stoppered burette for lime water, a cup, a glass stirring rod, and a medicine dropper, a bottle of full-strength lime water, and a bottle of phenolphthalein. The method of operating is to measure with the burette 20 c.c. of the cream to be tested into the cup, then rinse the burette with an equal quantity of rain water into the cup. Into this mixture put four drops of phenolphthalein indicator with the medicine dropper. Fill the 50 c.c. burette up to the top of the graduations with lime water. Let the lime water go into the cup slowly until the pink colour no longer disappears on stirring. The quantity of lime water taken to produce this permanent pink colour determines the amount of lactic acid present.

TEMPERATURE FOR CHURNING.

Generally 60 deg. may be quoted as the churning temperature If the temperature be too high an undue loss takes place in the buttermilk ; the butter will be soft, and cannot be readily handled, and the quality may be injured. If the temperature be too low, time is wasted in churning. It is always better to be a little low than high in temperature for churning. When fresh or sweet cream is churned the temperature needs to be lower in order to recover as much of the butter as possible. Equally good results are obtained at one place at 60 deg. as in another at 54 deg. at the same time of year. The proper temperature also varies slightly in the same places at different seasons—the range being about from 54 to 62 deg. Owing to the rise that takes place in temperature when churning, the cream needs to be lower in the summer as compared with the winter time. This variation is accounted for by the relationship or proportion that the liquid and solid fats in the butter bear to one another. The melting point of butter varies according to the pasture, the period of lactation of the cows, and the season of the year.

The buttermilk should be daily tested in all factories. In some apparently well-conducted places at the present day the loss sometimes amounts to 0·5, and even 1 per cent. of butter fat. Through carelessness, want of refrigerating power, or lack of opportunity to attend to this branch of the business, buttermilk is at times run away from the churns as rich in butter fat as new milk. On one occasion the buttermilk was kept from one churning of 1,200 lbs. of cream. The cream was unripe, and at too high a temperature. This buttermilk was properly ripened and cooled, then put back in the churn and churned again, when it yielded 108 lbs. of first-class butter ; and as there were four churnings a day at the factory the annual loss at this rate would be serious.

Once in a life-time is sufficient to meet with such an experience, and be impressed with the importance of keeping a check on the results of the churn.

Assurance has been given by factory managers on more than one occasion that if the value of the waste in skim-milk and buttermilk could be estimated since their companies started business, it would amount to more than was invested in buildings and plant ; in many cases to some thousands of pounds.

This state of affairs is almost at an end now, and directors of companies are every day recognising what their managers mean when they agitate for more refrigerating power. They are also becoming better acquainted with what constitutes the proper qualifications and duties of a manager. Unfortunately, there are still a few who think that a manager is engaged and paid more for his manual labour than for his brains and experience.

If a man works hard with his hands from daylight till dark, it is most unreasonable to expect him to study and look after those vital points upon which so much of their success depends.

CHURNING.

The churning should begin slowly, and if the churn has a tight lid the gas should be allowed to escape till its generation stops. Care should be taken that the speed of the churn is not so great as to carry round the cream without causing concussion. With ordinary box-churns 40 revolutions per minute are deemed fast enough. The churn should never be filled too full with cream ; two-thirds full is sufficient.

If the speed is too slow the process is needlessly prolonged. Practice will soon determine the proper speed to drive the churns at. Should the butter not come in half-an-hour, or thereabouts, the cream is not ripe enough, or it is too low in temperature, or there is too much of it in the churn, or the speed of the churn is too slow. When the cream is breaking cold water should be added, and all the corners rinsed down. The churning has to be continued till the butter is about between the size of sago and rice. As soon as the churn is stopped the buttermilk should be run off. If unnecessary delay takes place the milk coagulates and becomes difficult to get rid of.

When the buttermilk is run off more cold water should be added, and a few turns given to the churn, and then run off. Another rinsing ought to be sufficient. The main point to be studied in washing, or rather rinsing the butter in the churn, is to get the buttermilk away thoroughly and readily with the least possible quantity of water. The butter is then taken to be worked.

WORKING THE BUTTER.

A certain quantity—not more than the capacity of the machine—should be weighed and placed on the worker. After working the moisture out, $\frac{1}{2}$ ounce to the lb., or 3 per cent. of best dairy salt should be added. Many prefer to add 4 per cent. of salt. If the butter is intended to be kept for a considerable time a preservative may be added with the salt, but never more than one-half per cent. or $\frac{1}{2}$ lb. in 100 lbs. of butter.

Recent decisions in England indicate that it is injudicious on our part to have anything to do with preservatives, and where they are required the above proportion should not be exceeded. Some of our most successful factories have never used more than that quantity. The quantity of salt is arrived at by the taste of the consumers. If the market demands more or less salt, by all means supply that demand as long as the quality and prices are not jeopardized. The percentage of salt should always be arrived at by weighing both butter and salt so as to secure uniformity.

The working of the butter should distribute the salt evenly, and bring it in contact with all the particles in the first operation. That point is best determined by the number of revolutions of the worker, or by time. To arrive at the proper time, a number of samples may be taken off at intervals, then placed aside for 24 hours and examined. The samples showing streaks or unevenness in colour indicate that they have not been worked long enough.

The one that does not show unevenness in colour, and that has been on the worker for the shortest time, points out the time necessary. This time varies according to the style and speed of the worker in use, and slightly on the consistency of the butter. It must always be remembered that the salting should be thoroughly done in the first working, and the less working that will bring that about the better for the butter.

The butter should then be placed in a cool room till the next morning, and then put through the worker for the second time to remove surplus moisture before packing. Between the two workings it is not desirable to set the butter hard as it then receives a grinding on the worker that injures the texture. In packing, the tare of each box should always be taken—for local trade 56½ lbs. should be placed in the box, and 57 lbs. for export trade. The extra weight is to provide for a loss that takes place, and it insures the turning out of 56 lbs. when it reaches the retailer.

The butter should be firmly packed so that no air-holes are left in the butter, nor spaces in the corners or up the sides of the box. A good plan is to strip and examine a box of butter occasionally.

It is false economy to use inferior parchment paper for lining the butter-boxes. The boxes should be placed in the cool room, and the temperature reduced before sending away to market.

It is a comparatively easy matter to make a fair quality of butter under favorable conditions. It is a science to be able to make a choice butter possessing good keeping qualities under varying circumstances. The art of butter-making is yet in its progressive state. Our best specialists in the business are still learning something, and they all recognise that much remains to be learned, and as a strictly definite rule cannot be followed in butter-making each must adapt himself so as to secure best results under existing local conditions.

BUTTER-MAKING FOR FARMERS.

Much of the butter produced in the colony is made by farmers and dairymen who find it inconvenient or impossible to dispose of their milk to a creamery or factory. The proper handling of the milk, the treatment of the cream, and manufacture of butter demand consideration separate from that of the factory. As the average run of dairy butter on the market is of much lower quality than that from the factories, there would appear to exist a greater scope for improvement. But owing to many reasons the dairy butter can never hope to get on equal terms with factory output.

The chief obstacle in the way in our climate is the want of refrigeration. It will not pay small dairymen to bestow as much attention, or to provide as perfect appliances for manufacturing butter, as it does when treating it in a large way. In exceptional instances as good, and occasionally a better, article is made on the farm; but being small in quantity, it is confined purely to the local market.

When a surplus of dairy butter finds its way on the local market, it has to be disposed of at low figures, to allow for mixing up and making into large quantities of uniform quality that will warrant exporting. In some places this handicap can be overcome by the people combining and adopting the factory system.

Attention is specially directed to the regulations on another page regarding the care of milk and cream. Many hints are also given under the heading "Factory Butter-making."

The milk when set in dishes in hot weather often thickens before half the cream rises, and even under ordinary circumstances a greater percentage of the butter-fat is lost in the skim-milk by the gravity system than by the modern separator. Cleanliness and temperature are the great essential points to be studied for successful butter-making. The dairy should be so erected as to permit of its being easily kept clean and sweet, and the temperature regulated.

Every dairy should have a fire-place, or stove, to keep the place dry as well as to regulate the temperature during the winter. Small cheap refrigerators within the reach, and suitable for a small dairy, is a convenience not yet catered for. In the meantime the temperature of the dairy in the summer must be kept as low as possible. A temperature of 60 deg. is the average required, about 65 deg. is the best in winter, and 54 deg. in summer, but it is seldom practicable to get the dairy so low in hot weather.

Speaking of temperature, in how many dairies is a thermometer to be found ? A thermometer in a dairy is as great an essential as a compass on a ship.

A ship can be steered on her course without the aid of a compass, so can butter be made without a thermometer, but how much safer, and what a lot of energy, time, and trouble are saved by their use.

Every dairyman should possess a thermometer and use it. A proper one for the dairy costs 1s. or 1s. 6d. Those without any frame are best, as they can easily be kept clean. If it is set in a wooden frame, it ought to be removed before placing in the milk or cream. If the frame is put in the milk, it soon becomes foul.

The dairy is unfortunately too often considered a handy depôt in which to place all sorts of things. Sometimes a hare or rabbit is left hanging up. Often it is made to serve as a general cool room for fruit, vegetables, and meat.

Even in careful hands those things bring about flies and evil odours sometimes. Milk, cream, and butter are great absorbents of odours, and great damage is caused by exposing them to any objectionable smells.

It is not generally known that delicately scented pomades are made by exposing pure fat in thin layers to the scent of flowers. The fat absorbs and retains the beautiful odours.

The natural delicacy, aroma, and flavour of nice butter properly made should be preserved.

If those characteristics are spoiled in any way the value of the butter is reduced. The surroundings of the dairy should, therefore, be always kept clean and sweet.

The cream should be mixed always after each skimming is added, and churning should not take place sooner than twelve hours after the last lot has been mixed.

If the churning is done immediately after mixing, the older or riper cream comes into butter first, and the newer or more unripe cream is liable, and often does, run away with the buttermilk. As the matter of temperature is easily disposed of on paper, but often difficult to carry out in practice, it is perhaps better to dwell on it a little longer. To raise the temperature of the cream for churning the vessel containing it may be placed in a larger one which contains warm water. Stir the cream, and take it out when it reaches the desired heat. Never pour hot water into the cream to raise the temperature.

A well or stream of cool water is a great help on a farm. With cold water a great deal can be done. The cream can be reduced in the same way as pointed out above for raising the temperature by putting cold water in the outer vessel instead of hot. In most places it is the exception rather than the rule to have a supply of cold water. When ordinary means are not at hand, cream can be cooled by putting a wet bag or cloth round the vessel and placing it on a shallow pan of water in a draught of air over night.

Water can be reduced in the same manner for washing the butter. This plan was practised all through the past severe summer with good results. When a sultry close night was encountered a little salt was added to check the souring, and the cream was left over till the following night to be cooled. If there is no air in motion this plan of cooling is not effective. It is the rapid evaporation that causes the reduction in temperature. Water may also be cooled by dissolving a little salt and saltpetre in it quickly. A reduction of up to 10 deg. can be obtained by this means.

In some localities the only water to be had at times of the year is discoloured and muddy. A good easy plan for clearing such water will be found in Mr. Pearson's paper, read at the last meeting of the Factory Managers' Association, and referred to on another page.

For the churning, working, salting, packing, and other treatment of butter, the dairyman can be guided by the suggestions for factory butter-making. His attention is also directed to the chapter on the care of dairy utensils.

MILK TESTING.

SHORT INSTRUCTIONS.

There are three vital points in milk testing that must be recognised in order to insure reliable results. The first is to secure a proper representative sample of the milk to be tested. The second is to get a true sample from the composite test bottle into the test flask. And the third point includes careful attention to all the remaining details of working.

PREPARING THE SAMPLE BOTTLES.

Composite samples give reliable results, and save the trouble of daily testing. Special graduated bottles are in the market, and may be obtained very cheaply. Rubber corks should be used, as they are easily kept clean and sweet. Pure formalin is the most satisfactory preservative for keeping the samples. Four drops of formalin added with a medicine-dropper is sufficient to put in the composite bottle. The bottles should be thoroughly cleansed after each testing is done. For use on the farm, the names or numbers of the cows can be attached to the neck of the bottles, and at the creamery or factory the name or number of the supplier can be attached.

SECURING THE SAMPLES.

After a cow is milked, and the milk weighed, pour it from one bucket into another and then back before taking the sample. Immediately afterwards take some with a cup or measure, and put some into the composite bottle. The same quantity should be added each time, and at the end of each week the bottle will contain a representative sample of the milk for that period. In a factory or creamery the drip system is the most reliable.

MEASURING THE TEST SAMPLE.

The contents of the composite bottles should be thoroughly mixed. If the cream has set or is hard to mix, the bottles should be placed in warm water at a temperature of 120 deg. for a few minutes. The cream is then more easily dissolved and mixed with the milk. A bottle-extender greatly facilitates the mixing when the bottles are too full to shake. The sample is measured with a 17·6 c.c. capacity pipette, and put in the test flask. To prevent spilling, the flask should be held at an angle to allow the air to escape.

THE SULPHURIC ACID.

For milk-testing, sulphuric acid of 1·827 specific gravity is used. Special hydrometers for ascertaining the strength of the acid cost 3s. 6d. each, and a glass jar for holding the acid 1s. 6d. When using the hydrometer the temperature of the acid should be 60 deg. Fahr. Never put a metal or wooden frame thermometer in the acid, only glass or porcelain vessels should be used. The acid bottle should be kept corked when not in use, as it absorbs moisture from the air if exposed and becomes weak. The acid and milk ought to be about 70 deg. in temperature before mixing. It is neglect of temperature and strength of acid that causes a white curdy matter, or a black charred substance, to appear in the fat column. This temperature may be secured by placing the test bottles in a water bath of the desired heat after measuring. The acid may be cooled or heated in the same manner, but before measuring. Altering the strength or quantity of the acid is not recommended. All bottles containing sulphuric acid should have glass ground stoppers. The bottles should always be labelled "Poison," and kept out of the reach of children when not in use.

MEASURING THE ACID.

The acid is measured with a 17·5 c.c. glass measure, and poured down the inside of the neck of the test flask without disturbing the milk. The test flask should be held at an angle to allow the air to come out as the acid goes in, to prevent spilling. The test samples may be shaken separately by hand or together in a cradle. It is possible to dissolve the milk in less than the quantity of acid added, and sometimes a clear layer of acid remains at the bottom. This can be overcome by giving the bottles a good shaking with a reverse motion before finishing.

WHIRLING THE BOTTLES.

The speed at which the machine has to be turned depends on the gearing, and the diameter of the testers. If the bottle-wheel of the machine is 12 inches in diameter, that wheel should be made to turn 980 times per minute. If 18 inches in diameter, 800 revolutions per minute, and if 24 inches in diameter, 693 revolutions per minute. If the bottle-wheel is 18 inches in diameter, and geared to revolve ten times for one turn of the handle, the operator should turn the handle 80 times per minute to attain the necessary speed. If the bottle-wheel be geared by friction, care should be taken that no slipping takes place. For factory or creamery use the steam-turbine machines are far preferable to the others.

ADDING THE WATER.

After turning the tester for six minutes, hot water, 180 deg., is added up to the neck of the flasks. Rain or soft water should be used for this purpose. After adding the water the machine is turned for three minutes, then more water is added to bring the liquid up in the neck of the flask to between the 7 and 10 mark. Another minute's turning and the operation is complete. If only a few samples are to be tested, the water may be added with the milk pipette ; but where a large number have to be done a can with a rubber tube and pinch-cock is handiest.

READING THE TESTS.

A pair of fine-pointed dividers is of great assistance in taking the measurement of the fat column. The fat is measured from the lower line between it and the water to the top of the column. Having taken that span with the dividers, one point is placed at 0, and the other will show the percentage of fat on the scale on the neck of the bottle. Each large division represents 1 per cent., and each small space two-tenths or 0·2 of 1 per cent. In very cold weather the fat column often partly solidifies before a reading can take place. This may be prevented by keeping up the temperature of the samples. Hot water may be put in the pan of the machine, and the test flasks placed in warm water after whirling is finished, until the readings are recorded. This precaution is not necessary for the greater part of the year.

COMPUTING THE BUTTER CONTENTS.

In order to arrive at the commercial butter contents in milk per the respective butter-fat percentages, it is necessary to deduct a small loss that takes place in skimming, plus another loss that occurs in churning, and then add a percentage to make up for the usual quantity of water, curd, and salt contained in commercial butter. As the net addition is different with each test it is impracticable, as well as a waste of time, to work out each result by such a roundabout method. The following table of test values agrees with the Babcock table adopted by most of our factories. All milk should be reduced to butter, per its test, before quoting its money value. This system is more precise and equitable than differential rates per gallon, and is not liable to many misleading and complicated interpretations. Many useful hints, together with detailed instructions, are generally issued by the makers of each machine. Beginners should take a few lessons in the use of the Babcock tester from some one who has had experience.

VALUE OF TESTS. BABCOCK TESTER.

Tests.	Lbs. of Milk required to make 1 lb. Butter.	
	Correctly in Decimals.	Approximately in Fractions.
3·0	30·58	30½
3·1	29·58	29½
3·2	28·51	28½
3·3	27·62	27½
3·4	26·73	26¾
3·5	25·90	26
3·6	25·15	25
3·7	24·45	24½
3·8	23·74	23¾
3·9	23·12	23
4·0	22·52	22½
4·1	21·94	22
4·2	21·35	21¼
4·3	20·81	20¾
4·4	20·29	20¼
4·5	19·80	19¾
4·6	19·34	19¼
4·7	18·89	18¾
4·8	18·46	18½
4·9	18·06	18
5·0	17·67	17¾

To compute the number of pounds weight of butter contained in milk.

Divide the pounds and decimals of a pound, of milk agreeing with the test result, into the total number of pounds of milk.

Example—1,000 lbs. of milk tests 4·0 per cent. butter fat.

It will be seen above that it takes 22·52 lbs. of milk testing 4·0 to make one pound of butter.

Therefore :—22·52)1000·00(44·4
                        9008
                        ̄ ̄ ̄ ̄
                        9920
                        9008
                        ̄ ̄ ̄ ̄
                        9120
                        9008
                        ̄ ̄ ̄
                        112

44·4 lbs. of butter are computed to be contained in 1,000 lbs. of milk with a 4·0 test.

MONTHLY CHART.
for the guidance of Dairymen in recording each Cow's Milk.

NAMES OF COWS.	1	2	3	4	5	6	7	8	9	10	11	12	13	14	15	16	17	18	19	20	21	22	23	24
DATE	LBS. MILK	LBS. MILK	LBS. MILK	LBS. MILK	LBS. MILK	LBS. MILK	LBS. MILK	LBS. MILK	LBS. MILK	LBS. MILK	LBS. MILK	LBS. MILK	LBS. MILK	LBS. MILK	LBS. MILK	LBS. MILK	LBS. MILK	LBS. MILK	LBS. MILK	LBS. MILK	LBS. MILK	LBS. MILK	LBS. MILK	LBS. MILK
1																								
2																								
3																								
4																								
5																								
6																								
7																								
8																								
9																								
10																								
11																								
12																								
13																								
14																								
15																								
16																								
17																								
18																								
19																								
20																								
21																								
22																								
23																								
24																								
25																								
26																								
27																								
28																								
29																								
30																								
31																								
TOTAL																								
TESTS. 1ST WEEK																								
2ND "																								
3RD "																								
4TH "																								
AVERAGE																								

SCALE :—ONE-THIRD OF PRACTICAL SIZE.

COW LEDGER FOR RECORDING EACH COW'S MILK FOR
THE YEAR.

BEAUTY.

(Calved 26.7.97.)

Month.	Milk.	Test.	Butter.	Price.	Value.		
1897.	gals.				£	s.	d.
July							
August ...	146	3·4	54·6	8d.	1	16	4
September ...	152	3·4	56·8	„	1	17	10
October ...	142	3·5	54·8	„	1	16	6
November ...	128	3·5	49·4	„	1	12	11
December ...	116	3·6	46·1	7d.	1	6	10
1898. January ...	97	3·7	39·6	„	1	3	·1
February ...	52	4·0	23	8d.	0	15	4
March ...	34	4·1	15·9	1s.	0	15	10
April ...	12	4·3	5·7	„	0	5	8
May							
June... ...							
TOTAL ...	879	...	345·9	...	11	10	4

THE UTILITY OF TESTING COWS.

The accompanying table of the actual return of a small dairy herd of Victorian cows has been compiled with a view of impressing on dairymen the great advantage to be derived from recording the results from each and every cow.

It is all very well to judge a cow by appearances, but practical men are well aware that many a fine-looking cow is unprofitable for the dairy. At the present time it is fully recognised that there is no way so reliable to tell a good cow from a bad one as a scales and Babcock tester. The average Victorian cow has the reputation of giving a very small return as compared with the cows of many other countries. Whether this is so or not is open to question, and would be a difficult query to settle definitely.

From previous records it would appear that Victoria possesses some cows almost as good as are to be found in any part of the world. No doubt the greater number are anything but profitable for dairying.

If bad cows were known for certain and weeded out, and the remaining cows received better attention, our prospects would be bright indeed in the dairying line.

Description of Herd.

The herd of cows under review is a cross-bred one. There is more shorthorn blood in them than anything else. About three-quarters shorthorn and the rest a mixture, but no Channel Island blood whatever.

Method of Treatment.

They did not receive any special attention. Each cow was treated alike, and they were all pastured together. With the exception of a limited supply of small potatoes for a few weeks, the cows had nothing but straw in addition to pasture. In common with the herds in many parts of the colony last season, this one was reduced to skin and bone for some months.

As a consequence the cows did not, at their best, give more than three-fourths of the yield of a normal season. They were kept in the Koroit district, and the dairy formed an auxiliary to other branches of farming.

Cows going out of milk at the beginning of the year and disposed of are not included. Neither are heifers coming in before the close of the year. All cows are quoted that could be said were on the farm the year round. Some of those milked for six months and others up to eleven months.

A VICTORIAN HERD.

SUMMARY OF RETURNS FOR YEAR ENDED 31st DECEMBER, 1897.

(Compiled by R. Crowe.)

No.	Name.	Milk.	Test.	Butter.	Price.	Value.		
		gallons.		lbs.	d.	£	s.	d.
1	Caroline	697	4·2	326·41	8	10	17	7
2	Star	641	4·2	300·18	8	10	0	1
3	Spot	630	4·2	295·03	8	9	16	8
4	Lottie	683	3·6	271·55	8	9	1	0
5	Bess	531	4·5	268·04	8	8	18	8
6	Kitty	563	4·2	263·65	8	8	15	9
7	Lily	509	4·6	263·15	8	8	15	5
8	Stumpy	732	3·2	256·63	8	8	11	1
9	Fanny	575	4·0	255·24	8	8	10	1
10	Flo	697	3·3	252·31	8	8	8	2
11	Bawley	619	3·6	246·12	8	8	4	0
12	Mary Ann ...	662	3·3	239·64	8	7	19	9
13	Jenny	670	3·2	234·89	8	7	16	7
14	Blossom	666	3·2	233·49	8	7	15	7
15	Polly	587	3·6	233·38	8	7	15	7
16	Snaily	521	4·0	231·27	8	7	14	2
17	Judy	502	3·8	211·44	8	7	0	11
18	Rosy	594	3·2	208·24	8	6	18	9
19	Lady	435	3·9	188·13	8	6	5	5
20	Bonny	430	3·9	185·97	8	6	3	11
21	Dolly	421	3·8	177·32	8	5	18	2
22	Molly	392	4·0	174·01	8	5	16	0
23	Matilda	492	3·2	172·48	8	5	14	11
24	Liz	399	3·8	168·05	8	5	12	0
25	Princess	409	3·7	167·28	8	5	11	6
26	Betty	385	3·9	166·56	8	5	11	0
27	Cherry	375	4·0	166·46	8	5	10	11
28	Nelly	471	3·2	165·12	8	5	10	0
29	Violet	359	3·8	151·20	8	5	0	9
30	Gloss	347	3·8	146·15	8	4	17	5
31	Redmond	365	3·6	145·11	8	4	16	8
32	Pansy	299	3·7	122·29	8	4	1	6
		16,658	...	6,886·79	...	229	10	0

ANALYSIS OF SUMMARY.

The average number of pounds of milk required to make a pound of butter was 24·19.

The average return in milk per head was 520 gallons, of butter 215·21 lbs., and in money £7 3s. 5d.

The return in milk from the best cow was 697 gallons, from the ten best an average of 625 gallons, from the ten worst an average of 390 gallons, and from the worst cow 299 gallons.

The return in butter from the best cow was 326·41 lbs., from the ten best an average of 275·21 lbs., from the ten worst an average of 157·07 lbs., and from the worst cow 122·29 lbs.

The return in money from the best cow is £10 17s. 7d., from the ten best an average of £9 3s. 5d., from the ten worst an average of £5 4s. 8d., and from the worst cow £4 1s. 6d.

STRIKING DEDUCTIONS.

In order to make the lesson more instructive, it is assumed that the cost of each cow's keep for a year amounts to £2 10s., and the cost of attention to £1 10s. This £4 is estimated to sufficiently provide for rent or interest on the investment for each cow's keep, and the labour involved. Anything returned over that sum may be looked upon as profit.

Therefore the best cow gives a profit of £6 17s. 7d., the ten best average £5 3s. 5d., the ten worst average £1 4s. 8d., and the worst cow a profit of 1s. 6d. The best cow gives over 91 times as much profit as the worst one, and the profit from the ten best cows amounts to nearly the gross return from the ten worst cows.

AN INTERESTING COMPARISON.

Many dairymen believe in cows that give a large quantity of milk ; others believe only in cows that give a good test. Both are right to a certain degree, and to be safe, the quantity as well as the quality must be taken into account.

Attention is directed to the two cows, Nos. 7 and 8. The latter gives 223 gallons more milk than the former and yet brings in less money. Both are almost equally profitable cows, although one gives a 4·6 test and the other only 3·2. The goal can really be secured by widely-differing routes.

ANOTHER COMPARISON.

In looking over the monthly charts containing the records of those cows, it is found that "Lady," No. 19, gives the largest quantity for that period. The following monthly comparison is interesting :—

No.	Galls. Milk.	Test.	Butter.	Price.	Value.
19	140	3·7	57·26	8d.	£1 18 2
2	89	3·7	36·40	8d.	£1 4 3

The best return for a month by cow No. 2 is quoted, and in the monthly comparison No. 19 cow would get credit for being by far the more profitable animal. However, in looking at the year's record it is found that she was only a sprinter. For the month No. 19 gives 13s. 11d. more than No. 2, but for the year No. 2 gives-

£3 14s. 8d. more than No. 19. The one cow gave a big yield for a short period. The other did not give a big flow, but was a consistent milker, and came out best.

CHEAPENING COST OF PRODUCTION.

If it costs £4 to produce 326 lbs. of butter with the best cow and the same amount to produce 122 lbs. of butter with the worst cow, then it has cost less than 3d. per lb. to produce butter from the good cow and almost 8d. per lb. with the bad one.

A PROBLEM.

A herd that would give an average return of £7 3s. 5d. under such conditions, and in a year described by the oldest residents as the worst experienced for 30 years past, would be designated a picked herd. Therefore, this may be termed a picked herd, and if the individual members of a picked herd vary so much in the returns given by them, it would be most interesting to know to what extent the results of an average herd would differ when recorded in the same way.

GREAT POSSIBILITIES.

If such returns can be obtained under such adverse circumstances by an ordinary or mixed herd of cows in Victoria, what is it possible to secure from a herd, say, like the ten best cows in a favorable year? It is said that the average return from Victorian cows is 290 gallons—not equal to that of the worst cow here quoted. The ten best cows gave two and a quarter times that of the worst cow, so it can easily be seen what scope for improvement lies in this direction.

If it has been worth our while building up an industry of the magnitude—local and export—of £2,500,000 with the indifferent cows we are credited with, it will not be a hard matter to more than hold our own against all countries in the world if we pay more attention to the breeding, feeding, and management of our cattle. To say that we are not making headway in this direction would not be true. In every district there are to be found a few up-to-date dairymen, who serve as splendid examples to the remainder, and who are ever ready to adopt improved methods. This system of recording the quantity of each cow's milk, together with the quality, is strongly recommended. The beginning is the hardest part of it. Give the plan a trial, and you will find the trouble or delay not nearly so much as it appears. In a short time it will become part of the routine of milking, and the information continually gained will far outweigh the little extra attention. What better technical education can be afforded the young people who usually do the milking; and what a splendid thing it is to know definitely which cows are worth keeping and breeding from.

CARE OF DAIRY UTENSILS.

All cans and vessels of tin in which milk has been used should be rinsed out with cold water first, then washed with hot water, and afterwards scalded with boiling water or steam. If scalding water is used first, the albumen in the remaining milk sticks fast to the tin and renders the operation of cleansing most difficult.

Wooden vessels should receive almost the same treatment. Churns and butter-workers should have all the small particles of butter washed down with cold water after use, and then scrubbed and scalded. Should hot water be used first, the little waste atoms melt on the wood, and are sometimes liable to soak in.

If the wood is once allowed to become greasy in this manner it is almost impossible to' again get it back into good working order. The frequent use of lime-water cannot be too strongly recommended for all milk and butter appliances, churns in particular. Many instances are known where contaminated vessels have caused hundreds of pounds worth of loss to the producers, therefore, proper attention should be bestowed on cleanliness to insure best results.

PURIFYING WATER.

In the northern districts of the colony it is the exception, rather than the rule, to have a supply of clean pure water suitable for washing butter. Mr. Pearson, Government Agricultural Chemist, explained a simple process of treatment for muddy or discoloured water, at the Conference of the Australasian Butter and Cheese Factories Managers' Association, May, 1897. Two tanks are used, one above the other. The upper one is used for the clarification of the water, and the lower one is for the reception of the clarified water. The top tank is fitted with a tap at the lowest point of the bottom. Let us suppose that 500 gallons of clear water are required for use each day; then it will be necessary to have those two tanks of 500 gallons capacity each. Two vessels of any convenient size are necessary to contain a supply of soda and alum solutions; also a watering-can for measuring the liquid. Fifty gallons is a handy size for the former vessels. The alum solution is of such a strength that one measureful of it will convey to the 500-gallon tank 12 grains of alum per gallon, or 6,000 grains altogether. As there are 7,000 grains to the 1 lb. avoirdupois, that would be six-sevenths of a pound. If the measuring-can holds 1 gallon, then the amount of alum to be put into the 50-gallon vessel would be 43 lbs. That would be sufficient to last for 50 days. The amount of soda should be about 9 grains per gallon; that is to say, the strength of the soda solution should be three-quarters that of the alum solution. Thus, if 43 lbs. of alum were put into 50·

gallons, about 33 lbs. of soda should be dissolved in the other 50-gallon vessel. The process is simple. Fill the top tank with water in the afternoon. The measureful of alum solution is then evenly distributed over the surface of the water by means of the rose of the watering-can. The alum solution is then stirred into the water with a stirrer, this being done gently and carefully, so as not to get any air bubbles into the water. About ten minutes afterwards the measureful of soda solution is distributed through the water in the same way, stirring carefully as before. In the morning it will be found that the alumina has been entirely precipitated, and has settled on the bottom of the tank, carrying with it the solid impurities, including bacteria, from the water, and leaving the water in the tank absolutely clear and limpid. A siphon should then be carefully introduced, so as not to stir up the mud at the bottom, and the clear water should be removed into the lower tank, where, if required, it could be cooled for use when necessary.

Under the orifice of the siphon is a tin plate attached to the siphon pipe about 10 in. or 12 in. in diameter, which prevents the water from taking up with it as it passes into the siphon any sediment from the bottom of the tank.

When empty the top tank is sluiced out through the tap, and the whole operation is gone through as before.

Mr. Pearson states that this is an old-fashioned process, but recent investigations have shown that it is as efficient as any known process of purifying water. Alum used to the extent of from 12 to 20 grains per gallon has been found to result in complete sterilization of water—that is to say, in the perfect removal of bacteria. Some who have seen this process at work have greatly admired the appearance of the water, but have expressed a fear that by using alum they would be introducing an injurious substance into the butter, in the manufacture of which the water was used. This fear is groundless, because, as already explained, the whole of the alumina is separated in the form of precipitate. It is, in fact, by virtue of this precipitation of the alum, and the conveyance in the precipitate of all the impurities, that the clarification takes place. But even supposing that a little of the alum were to be left in the water, a very simple calculation will show that the amount thereby introduced into the butter would be infinitesimal. The amount of water in butter is about 10 per cent., so that 1 cwt. of butter would contain about 11 lbs. (a little over 1 gallon) of water. As 1 gallon of water receives only 12 grains of alum, even if all the alum that was put in were to remain in the water, the amount conveyed to the butter would be not more than 13 grains to the cwt. As a matter of fact, even if only partial precipitation of the alum were to take place, there could be only 2 or 3 grains of alum left in a gallon of water, so that there would never be any fear of more than 2 or 3 grains of alum to the cwt. of butter. It will be seen that those 2 or 3 grains of possible addition of alum are too insignificant to be considered.

When once the process is seen in operation it will be found so very simple and so very easy of application that is unlikely that any one troubled with impure water would hesitate to adopt it.

RULES FOR MILK AND CREAM SUPPLY.

The quality of the butter made in this colony largely depends on the care bestowed on the production and treatment of the milk and cream before being manufactured. In the interests of the dairying industry it is necessary for the producers to exercise every precaution to insure the production of a first-class quality of butter. This fact is recognised by most dairymen, but there are some who do not give due attention to these matters.

It is to be regretted that it is not possible to deliver all the milk produced to the creameries and factories, and it is deplorable to find many who are within easy reach of a creamery or factory trying to separate the milk from their own cows and manufacture their butter in small lots.

Perhaps the worst results are obtained from cream separated on the farms and kept until too old before being delivered to the place of manufacture. The cause for complaint is not due to the use of small separators, but to the want of proper conveniences and accommodation, and, the lots being small, the necessary care is not given to the cream.

In our warm climate it is absolutely essential to have the aid of refrigeration at times of the year in order to make best butter.

In the absence of refrigeration the quality of the output is irregular, so, in order to attain and keep up uniformity, the milk should be delivered to where it can be treated in large quantities and manipulated to best advantage.

With a view to encouraging an improvement on the existing conditions, the following rules have been suggested by the dairy experts connected with this Department as a] guide to dairymen :—

RULES.

Care of Milk.

1st. The pastures, yards, and surroundings should be kept clean and free from carrion, and all decaying matter which may cause noxious smells.

2nd. Milk should be used and supplied only from healthy cows, which are fed on wholesome food, and have access to plenty of pure water.

3rd. In districts where sufficient salt is not naturally available a moderate allowance should be provided, as it adds to the health of the cattle and to the quality of the milk.

4th. Provide shelter for the cows against excessive heat and cold, and the flow and quality of the milk will be better.

5th. Be sure and make provision against the dry season by providing green crops, in order to prolong the period of milking and maintain the health and condition of your cattle.

6th. Treat the cows kindly; milk them thoroughly and with regularity, that they may cultivate a milching habit.

7th. Milk should be drawn from the cows in a cleanly manner, the udders should be brushed or washed; milking with dry hands is preferable to the practice of dipping the fingers into the milk to moisten them.

8th. Immediately after the milk has been drawn from the cow it should be strained through a wire or cloth strainer.

9th. All buckets, cans, and other utensils with which the milk is brought into contact should be of tin; rusty vessels should be discarded.

10th. The milk vessels should be kept clean and sweet and washed with cold or tepid water first, then scalded with boiling water, and finished with a rinsing of limewater; they should afterwards be drained out, sunned, and aired. Milk cans should not be left bottom upwards.

11th. The milk should be aerated, by dipping, pouring, or stirring, or by use of an aerator. After the milk has been aired it should be cooled quickly to as low a temperature as possible; and this should be done in a clean place where there is no dust or smell.

12th. The milk should be kept in a place where the atmosphere is free from foul or injurious smells. Milk that is left without the shelter of some roof should be protected from sun and rain by placing the lid on the can upside down, or by some other efficacious means.

13th. Every dairyman should have a thermometer, and know the difference between the temperature of the atmosphere and water; the cans of milk should be kept in the coolest place.

14th. The night and mornings' supplies of milk should be kept in separate vessels, and may be mixed, when cooled to the same temperature, at the creamery or factory.

15th. "Biestings," or milk from newly-calved cows, should not be sent to the factory or creamery, nor separated till after the eighth milking. The milk of some such cows is not fit for butter-making for a much longer period, and should not be sent until it is in fit condition.

(Suppliers infringing this rule should incur a heavy penalty.)

16th. Each supplier should furnish pure sweet milk to which nothing has been added and from which no part has been removed.

17th. The factory or creamery manager should reject any milk which he considers unfit for use in the manufacture of the finest quality of butter, and his directors should assist in carrying out this recommendation.

Care of Cream.

18th. The cream should be cooled to as low a temperature as possible immediately after separating, and well stirred at least three times a day.

19th. The morning and night's cream should not be mixed till after each has reached the same temperature.

20th. The cream should be delivered to the factory daily in warm weather, in the coolest part of the day if possible, and at no time should it be kept at the dairy longer than two days.

21st. A little salt may be used in hot weather to assist in keeping cream in good condition.

22nd. The cream cans should be covered from the sun in transit, and sliplids used to prevent churning.

23rd. Use a "Babcock" milk-tester, and know exactly what each cow in your herd gives you per year; turn off the unprofitable cows and replace them with good ones.

If the foregoing rules are adhered to, the value of our products will be enhanced and the profits of the milk producer increased.

Testing Milk for Factories, Creameries, and Milk Suppliers.

In case of disputes arising between milk suppliers and managers of butter factories and creameries regarding the percentage of butter fat contained in any supplier's milk the expert attached to the dairy section of the Department will test samples of milk free of cost by either visiting the factories or creameries, or receiving a sample of milk that has been collected by the "drip" system by the manager and testing it in the Department's laboratory, Melbourne.

Dairy farmers desirous of receiving instructions in the process of testing milk by the "Babcock" tester, by applying to the Secretary for Agriculture will be taught in Melbourne the proper method of using the appliances necessary for that purpose by the Department's experts.

LIST OF SHIPPING CHARGES FOR PRODUCE SHIPPED THROUGH THE DEPARTMENT OF AGRICULTURE.

Butter	...	...	...	per box, 2d.
Chickens	...	...	...	per pair, 5d.
Ducks	...	...	...	,, 5d.
Eggs	...	...	...	per dozen, 1d.
Geese	...	...	...	per pair, 9d.
Hares	...	...	...	,, 3d.
Mutton	...	...	...	per carcass, 8d.
Pork	...	...	...	,, 8d.
Rabbits	...	...	...	per pair, 2d.
Turkeys	...	...	...	,, 9d.

The above charges to be paid by the shipper or his agent, together with freight, &c., before obtaining delivery of bills of lading.

PASTEURIZING.

In order to understand the pasteurizing system of treating milk or cream for butter-making purposes, it is necessary to have a knowledge of the composition of milk and its relation to bacteria. Milk is a complex food, and is composed principally of water, fat, caseine, sugar, and ash, in the following average proportions :—

Water	...	...	...	86·80
Fat	...	...	...	3·70
Caseine and albumen	...	...	3·75
Sugar	...	...	...	5·00
Ash	...	...	...	0·75

Two great objects are sought in the pasteurizing of milk or cream. The first is to drive off the obnoxious gases that are present in milk produced from certain fodders, such as rape, lucerne, &c. Such milk has a strong undesirable odour, usually termed as " cowy." It has been found that by proper aeration this fault is easily got rid of, but for some reason or other the farmer has not taken to aeration.

In order to be effective, the aeration of milk must be carried out at a high rate of temperature after coming from the cow and before the undesirable element becomes fixed in the milk. Since the milk producer has not undertaken this easy precaution in regard to the welfare of his milk supply for butter-making, it is therefore compulsory to effect the desired object at a later period —that is, when it reaches the creamery or factory. As the milk generally arrives comparatively cold at the creameries, it is not possible to get the objectionable volatile elements liberated without raising the temperature. It is found that the pasteurizing of the milk and the later exposure of it on the cooler to the atmosphere effected the object sought for by aeration.

As a matter of fact, it appears that greater good has been achieved from this point of view than from a bacterial standpoint. All the experiments so far conducted prove that the greatest success in improvement of quality is noticeable only in districts that produce milk off of rich artificial grass pastures. It is still doubtful whether pasteurization will effect any improvement in butter made under good conditions from milk produced on clean hard pastures.

The second object looked for is to kill all the active microorganisms that develop in the milk after it leaves the cow. Hitherto this has been the only consideration dwelt upon by scientists. It is well known that the milk in the udder of a healthy cow contains no bacteria. Many experiments have proved conclusively that such is a fact, and that all the changes that subsequently take place in the milk are due to the growth of bacteria. In ordinary dairying it is impossible to take milk from the cow without bringing a certain amount of bacteria with it into the bucket. Their presence is universal. They are in the air, in dust, in the soil, and in the water. Their chief function is to break up substances or bodies for the use of living animals or plants. Under favorable conditions bacteria multiply at an enormous rate. Milk is an excellent medium for their propagation.

Usually a certain class of bacteria acts upon the milk-sugar and converts it into lactic acid; this acid gives the sour taste and thickens the milk. This is looked upon by the milk producer as prejudicial, and yet the butter-maker, in order to bring about the changes necessary in the cream before making good butter, has to make overtures to and encourage the same class of bacteria by supplying the requisite conditions for their development. The results in the past were very uncertain owing to the want of knowledge that existed in regard to this then unknown power. As well as the friendly bacteria getting into the milk and cream, very often unfriendly characters find their way in also. The number of unfriendly germs are sometimes present to such an extent that an evil result must ensue. The surroundings are always responsible for this state of affairs. If the milking yards are dirty and dusty, or the cows and milk vessels not properly cleaned, the result cannot be otherwise than bad. It is to kill the undesirable organisms that pasteurization is intended.

PASTEURIZING MILK OR CREAM FOR BUTTER-MAKING.

Pasteurizing milk or cream to obtain a superior butter is the latest development of dairying. Still we cannot by any means call it a new discovery, for there is nothing new in heating milk to 155 deg. to get rid of bad odours caused mostly by artificial

feeding of various sorts and qualities. A similar system was practised by the dairy people of Devonshire and Cornwall 500 or 600
years ago, for who has not heard of Devonshire scalded cream?
In two important points, however, their system and ours differ, viz.,
in those old times, after the milk was heated to a high temperature it was allowed to cool in the pans without artificial means,
while in ours it is cooled by refrigerating machinery at once to
60 deg. or lower, by this means solidifying the fatty globules in
the milk, and thus when the cream is churned insuring a good
grained as well as a sound keeping butter.

Another important change from the old system is that whereas
the milk was allowed to stand till the cream gathered and ripened,
which did not take place for three or four days, sometimes longer,
now by putting in a quantity of "ferment" or "ripener" in the
cream it is ready for churning in 24 hours, or before any dele-
terious bacteria gets back again in the cream.

The following is a description of the process practised at
present in our factories. Taking for granted you have got the
milk into your dairy or factory in a sweet and sound condition,
and that you have a pasteurizing plant fitted up to date, you then
run the milk through the separator, making the cream a little
thinner than usual. From the separator the cream runs into the
heater; watch that the temperature of the cream does not rise
higher than 155 deg. From the heater the cream passes on to
the cooler, which, with the aid of the refrigerator or ice, will bring
it back to 60 deg., or lower if required. The ferment, or starter,
is now added. The quantity required of this starter is from 5 to
10 per cent., according to the amount of acidity in it and the
time at which it is intended to churn.

How to obtain the Ferment or Ripener.

The European system is, take 1 gallon of sweet skim-milk and
heat it to 155 deg. Fahr., and then cool the milk quickly to 90 deg.;
then add to it a bottle of the cultivated ferment which is now imported from America, Denmark, and Sweden. This done, place
the milk in a water bath at 90 deg. and leave it for eighteen
hours. This milk must be covered with a thin butter-cloth only.
After this the milk will be thick. It then has to be cooled down
to 60 deg. in cool water and left alone without stirring. Only
the top of it has to be skimmed off before use. The ferment
is then ready for ripening the cream, which is now kept at a temperature of about 60 deg. If everything be right the cream
should be churned in 24 hours, and the butter afterwards treated
in the usual way.

The 1 gallon mentioned previously will be sufficient for ripening 20 gallons of cream. Of this ferment you must take 1 quart
for making the "acidifier" for the following day, which is done

in the following manner:—Take 1 gallon of fresh skim-milk and heat it up to 155 deg. Fahr.; then cool to 90 deg.; add the quart of sour milk, and leave it for six or seven hours. Then the 1 gallon and the 1 quart of milk is ready for ripening the cream next day. If the result of this ferment turns out good butter you may continue this ripener for some time before fresh lactic ferment is required.

Victorian System.

Perhaps it may be advisable to give experiences here of obtaining this ripener or ferment, because it is very often found that a successful dairy system in a cool climate is often the opposite in a hot one. For instance, experience has taught us that very little of the imported "ferment" is sound on its arrival here, as it will not stand age and long carriage. It has therefore been found necessary to make our own ripener just in a similar way to what has been already described, but with this slight difference, that whereas some of the European dairymen start with a scientifically cultivated "ferment" we start with a sound new milk instead of skim-milk, which in our climate often becomes deteriorated before arriving at that stage. However, much attention has of late been given to the preparation and use of cultivated ferments, and doubtless in the near future we will be able to send out for use pure cultures that can be relied upon to give satisfaction.

When a manager wants to change his starter his easiest and best plan is to obtain a litle buttermilk from an adjoining factory making a first-class butter. Then the churning and the usual process of manufacturing butter for market may be adopted. Before finishing this subject, it may be added that Messrs. A. N. Pearson and the dairy experts have for the last four years been experimenting in several of our factories, advising and demonstrating to the managers this system of butter-making, proving the merits of the method when the butter goes off flavour, and have succeeded in curing the faulty cream coming from a large number of creameries; but from some reason yet to be found out, the factory and creamery managers do not always keep the quality of the cream, after being pasteurized, up to the required standard.

We have also frequently exported a portion of the butter made at four of our best factories, but, with the exception of one, it cannot be said that the prices obtained have been as yet much above the average price obtained for butter made in the usual way. Probably our hot seasons and dried-up pastures, also long distance of carriage of milk from farm to factory, may militate against the complete success of this system being adopted in Victoria. Still it is recommended, where consumers' complaints about the quality of butter are numerous—and there are few factories where such are not rare—to make butter by this plan, in order to overcome the difficulty. There is no doubt that, as the system of pasteurizing becomes better understood by managers, superior results will be achieved ; and now that the method has been given an impetus it is expected most of the factories in the colony will be pasteurizing their outputs within another season or so. Particulars as to cost, &c., of pasteurizing plants may be obtained from any of the leading suppliers of dairy appliances in Melbourne.

CHEESE.

Canadian-Cheddar Cheese.

The unsatisfactory prices that have been obtained in England for cheese during the past two seasons have resulted in our dairy farmers losing sight, to a very large extent, of the importance of always being ready, in the event of a sudden fall in autumn in the value of butter, to convert the greater part of the milk into cheese.

So long as prices for butter in London continue remunerative, cheese-making for export will be a neglected industry in Victoria, but prices are not always going to remain as profitable for butter as they have been during the past two years. We have had three dry seasons in succession in Victoria, and owing to the scarcity of butter, the usual fall in value at the end of each of the past shipping seasons did not take place. But we are not always going to have dry seasons. Already there are indications that the season 1898-9 is going to be the best experienced since 1894-5, and should the present favorable prospects continue, there will be a large supply of milk next autumn.

Do the proprietors of butter factories realize what a heavy autumn supply of milk means? We are inclined to think that they seldom give much thought to the matter. Having passed through three dry seasons, it is quite probable that there may now be a run of good seasons. If so, the annual production of milk will be enormous. Additional land is being devoted to dairying every year, and new factories and creameries are being erected to deal with the increased supply of milk that will certainly be available.

A warning is necessary at the present juncture, and it is considered essential to point out to milk-growers not only the rock that looms in the distance, but also the means whereby that rock may be avoided.

The probable export season for butter terminates about the end of April in each year. Butter exported in May would arrive in England right in the middle of their flush season for milk, and the prices obtainable at that time of year for best Victorian factory butter would not be sufficiently high to enable our factories to pay more than, say, 2d. per gallon for milk, perhaps not so much.

Given, then, that we have a moist spring and a favorable summer, the supply of milk during February, March, April, and May will produce more butter several times over than will be required for Australian consumption. This will mean that prices here will probably fall below 6d. per lb. for prime quality. All below prime quality will have to be sold at an unprofitable figure. Prices for milk will be so low that dairy farmers might become disgusted with their occupation, and suddenly abandon dairying, and sway round to some other occupation that just at the time might be offering better prospects. Such a state of affairs would be calamitous both to the individual and to this country generally ; but how is it to be avoided ? Simply by combining cheese-making with butter-making at all our leading factories. This is the only way out of the difficulty, and if neglected the result will be serious for the dairying industry.

In England there is, as a rule, a fairly good market for good Cheddar cheese during the months of February, March, April, and May. The price, of course, will not leave as good a margin of profit as we have been getting for butter during the past three seasons, but the price which good cheese will realize, if shipped at the right time, will pay dairy farmers very much better than glutting the Melbourne and English markets with butter during the summer and autumn. It is, therefore, advisable for factories to be in a position to convert milk either into butter or cheese as the requirements of the world's markets may demand. By thus being able to manufacture cheese when butter is low, and *vice versâ*, gluts will, as far as possible, be minimized, and sudden fluctuations in the value of milk avoided.

Having so strongly recommended cheese-making during the summer months as the best possible means of avoiding a glutted butter market in the autumn, milk-growers will naturally expect some plain practical instruction regarding the latest and most approved methods of making cheese by this Canadian-Chedder system.

Pure Clean Milk necessary.

Before a factory makes arrangements to commence cheese-making there should be some guarantee that none but the very purest and cleanest milk shall be supplied. Purity and cleanliness in milk is far more necessary for cheese-making than for butter-making, although for both it should always be clean and pure. Begin by prevailing upon the milk suppliers to have clean cowsheds, to clean the cows' udders before milking, and to always keep their hands clean. A beginning must be made at the fountain head, because unless the strictest cleanliness be observed at every stage, from the time the milk is drawn from the cow until it is delivered to the cheese-maker, it is impossible for a good quality of cheese to be manufactured. There is altogether too much indifference amongst our milk-producers regarding this question of cleanliness. If anything like a correct estimate could be obtained of the depreciation in the value of our butter during one year owing to impurities in the milk and the want of cleanliness in handling it, the figures would have a startling effect on the community. Seeing that cheese requires purer milk and cleaner milk than butter, how very important, therefore, is it that all milk-suppliers, by supplying only the purest and cleanest of milk, should co-operate with the cheese-maker in producing a really prime article for the English market.

RECEIVING THE MILK.

Every can of milk that is intended for cheese should, before being accepted, be very closely scrutinized. Firmness on the part of the cheese-maker at this stage is of the utmost importance. Should there be the slightest shadow of suspicion as to either its sweetness, purity, or cleanliness, reject it at once. One can of unsuitable milk will destroy the whole of the milk received that morning. Why, then, should the milk of, say, nineteen careful milk suppliers be ruined just to accommodate one neglectful supplier who is too obstinate to acquire habits of cleanliness? Assuming the milk to be up to the required standard, it is received from the suppliers and strained into the large receiving vat, and gradually heated up to 86 deg. Fahr. The vat and the method of heating are so sufficiently well known that a description is unnecessary.

ADDING THE RENNET.

When to add the rennet is a stage in cheese-making that requires very careful attention. When the milk in the receiving vat has been brought to a temperature of 86 deg. Fahr., put about 5 ounces of it into a tea-cup. For this purpose have a graduated measuring glass, which only costs two shillings.

To the 5 ounces of milk add one teaspoonful of any good brand of artificial rennet. Stir the milk and the rennet together for five seconds and then watch for it to thicken. Should it thicken in from fourteen to seventeen seconds the milk in the vat will be ripe enough to "set," that is, to receive the rennet.

Sometimes, however, the milk does not thicken in from fourteen to seventeen seconds, and this happens in cold weather. The lowness of the surrounding temperature even when the milk is at 86 deg. Fahr. has been known to cause the milk to take 25 and in some cases 30 and 35 seconds to thicken. When this happens the temperature of the milk in the vat must be continued for a little while longer at 86 deg., or even increased a little, but on no account must it go over 90 deg. By waiting a few minutes, keeping the milk in the vat a little over 86 deg., it will ripen, despite the cold weather, when the fourteen to seventeen seconds test in the tea-cup will then come out all right.

The rennet must not be added until proof of the proper ripeness of the milk has been decided by the tea-cup test.

There is a very simple plan for telling the very moment when the milk in the cup has thickened, and beginners ought to make use of it. When the 5 ounces of milk are put in the cup, before adding the rennet put a small chip, say half-an-inch of a wooden match, or small piece of cork, into the milk, and then stir rapidly when adding the rennet. The little chip will whirl round with the milk, but the moment the milk thickens the chip will suddenly stop. By keeping a close eye on your watch the exact number of seconds from the adding of the rennet to the stopping of the chip is easily counted.

QUANTITY OF RENNET.

If good rennet is purchased the proper quantity to use is at the rate of 2 ounces for every 50 gallons of milk. This is the correct proportion. After thoroughly mixing the annatto with the milk then add the rennet. None but the best brands of rennet should be purchased. Stir the milk well for five minutes after adding the rennet, and then let it settle.

TESTING RENNET.

As rennet varies in quality its strength should be tested regularly. In factories every new supply ought to be tested. On farms where only a small quantity is used every bottle as it is opened should be tested before using. If the proportions stated in the standard referred to (a teaspoonful of rennet to 5 ounces of milk) does not thicken the milk in the cup in seventeen seconds in favorable weather, providing, of course, the milk is at the right temperature, then the rennet is weak in quality, and the proportion per 50 gallons of milk in the vat, as already explained, will have to be increased. Experience and observation soon enable even a beginner to determine the exact quantity of rennet to use even should the quantity vary a little in strength. The use of too much rennet must be guarded against. Too much rennet is one of the causes of "streaky" and of "bitter" cheese.

ANNATTO.

One ounce of annatto to every 50 gallons of milk will be sufficient. For cheese intended for export not more than half-an-ounce of annatto per 50 gallons of milk should be used, for the reason that the English consumer prefers a straw or lightly-coloured cheese. Add the annatto as soon as the test shows you the milk is ripe enough, and then stir well for five minutes so as to mix it evenly and thoroughly with the milk.

Cutting the Curd.

In about twelve minutes after the rennet has been added, the milk in the vat will have thickened or curded. A close watch must be kept so as to note the actual time the milk takes to curd. Having ascertained the actual number of minutes the milk took to curd, the time for cutting the curd will be two and a half times the number of minutes that elapsed from when the rennet was put in until the milk curded. Suppose, for instance, the milk takes twelve minutes to curd, in 30 minutes afterwards (*i.e.*, twice and a half times twelve) the curd is ready to cut. When everything goes on all right the "cutting" should commence from 40 to 42 minutes from the time when the rennet was added.

Here is an illustration showing how the whole operation actually works out.

Assume that the milk is ripe at a quarter to nine.

Add annatto at a quarter to nine, and stir the milk well until nine o'clock.

At nine o'clock add the rennet.

Stir the milk thoroughly until five minutes past nine.

At twelve minutes past nine the milk will be curds.

Thirty minutes afterwards (two and a half times twelve), *i.e.*, forty-two minutes past nine, the curd will be ready to cut.

By following this rule no mistake will be made as to the proper time for cutting the curd. Dipping the finger into the curd, a test adopted by many people, should be avoided.

How to Cut the Curd.

Extreme caution is required in cutting the curd, and care must be taken to avoid breaking or bruising it in any way, and the cutting must be cleanly done, leaving no bruised surface. The knives must cut well. There should no dragging, nor should there be any ragged surface on the curd when cut. First use the horizontal steel knife lengthwise, going from end to end of the vat, then use the vertical knife, going also from end to end. After this has been done then run the vertical knife through the curd across the vat, *i.e.*, from side to side. The curd should now be all in the size of about half-inch cubes.

Developing Acidity.

Having cut the curd, the next operation is for the development of acidity. Boiling water will now have to be used in order to raise the temperature of the whey up to 100 deg. Fahr. Before surrounding the vat with hot water it is always advisable to pass the hand gently round the sides and bottom of the vat so as to remove any curds that might be sticking there. It will take about 40 minutes to raise the temperature of the whey up to

100 deg. The curd meanwhile must be kept slowly stirred with a rake, with the teeth set wide apart so as not to cause any bruising. As the curd gets firmer stir faster, until 100 deg. has been gradually reached in the 40 minutes. When 100 deg. has been reached draw the hot water from the vat at once, and allow the curd to settle down for about an hour and a half, the vat meanwhile being covered in order to maintain an even temperature. At the expiration of the hour and a half sufficient acidity ought to be developed in the curd to permit of the whey being drawn off.

Testing the Curd for Acidity.

The only sure test for showing when the acidity is coming is the hot-iron one. Get a piece of half-inch iron and make it nearly, but not quite, red-hot. Take a handful of the curd, squeeze the whey out by compressing it gently, and then apply the hot iron to it. If when lifting the iron up from the curd it draws out fine hairy threads about one-eighth of an inch long it is time to draw the whey off and remove the curd to the cooler. If, however, the fine threads are not seen to be drawn up by the iron the curd must remain a little longer in the whey in order to reach the proper stage of acidity.

In the Cooler.

When the whey has been run off, remove the curd to the cooler. Let it remain without being disturbed for about ten minutes in order to give it time to " mat." After " matting " it is cut into squares for convenient handling, and also to permit of further drainage of any whey. Turn the curd every quarter of an hour for about an hour to an hour and a half. When the curd is placed in the cooler it is most important that the cooler, except when handling the curd, be covered with a sheet or piece of strong " duck," in order to maintain an even temperature and further develop the acidity.

After being from an hour to an hour and a half in the cooler, again apply the hot-iron test for acidity, when if the fine threads this time draw out fully three-quarters of an inch long, it will be time to put the curd through the curd cutter. If the fine threads do not come as described, turn the curd again, keep the cooler covered and wait a little longer. Developing the proper acidity and allowing the gases to escape are the secrets of success. If everything goes on alright the curd should not require to be in the cooler for more than from an hour and a quarter to an hour and a half, but at the very outside not more than an hour and 40 minutes.

The Curd Cutter.

The old curd mills that were used fifteen and twenty years ago are out of date. They used to bruise, tear, and grind the curd down too fine, thereby allowing the richness to escape, which reduces the quality of the cheese. The new style of curd cutter cuts, the curd as clean as you would cut chaff, instead of bruising it down as the old-fashioned curd mills did. The curd is only put through the cutter once, and it comes out in clean cut strips, each about 3 inches long by about half-an-inch in diameter. .

SALTING.

After putting the curd through the cutting machine it must be kept stirred and turned over now and again to prevent "matting," which operation also circulates the air through it, and cools it down to about 72 deg., at which temperature it is ready for salting. Add 1 lb. of salt for every 50 gallons milk that were in the vat. After mixing the salt thoroughly with the curd, give the curd another ten to fifteen minutes to allow the salt to properly dissolve before putting the curd into the "hoops" and pressing.

CHEESE PRESSES.

Where large quantities of cheese are made, such as in factories and on large dairy farms, the "gang" press should be used, but for small dairymen making only one or two cheeses a day, the ordinary screw press will do, as it saves the outlay for a "gang."

The "hoops" being made of galvanized iron and in four pieces, are one of the greatest improvements in modern cheese-making, as they entirely dispense with all the bother that used to be attached to the proper adjusting of lids and trimming the edges of the cheese.

Be careful not to press the curd hard the first half-hour, or the richness of the cheese will be lost. A sudden heavy pressure at first will also form a skin on the cheese which will prevent a free escape of whey and result in a "streaky" or a "mottled" cheese. Increase the pressure gradually after the lapse of half-an-hour. From fifteen to twenty hours, according to the size of the cheese, will be long enough for it to remain in the press. Then remove from the "hoops" and transfer direct to the shelves in the curing-room.

IN THE CURING-ROOM.

After cheese has been six weeks in the curing-room it will be ready for export to London. During the six weeks while the cheese is in the curing-room it will require to be "turned" once a day. Cheese intended for the Australian market need only be "turned" every second day until it is three months old, when it is fit for consumption. Uniformity of temperature is a very essential point in the curing-room. The temperature should, as far as possible, be maintained at about 66 deg.

CHEESE BANDAGES.

The imported seamless bandages are the best to use. Exporters of cheese to London should use no other. If, however, the ordinary cheese-cloth be used, sew it to suit the size of the "hoops" used, cut into required lengths, and then turn it inside out so that the seam will not show on the bandage on the outside. Always adjust the bandage on the hoop before filling with curd.

THE CHEESE PRESS.

All cheese factories and on farms where a large amount of cheese is made, the American gang press will be used. Small dairy farmers, who perhaps may not be making more than one or two cheeses daily, will find the old screw press answer the purpose just as well. The economy of the gang press is that it will press a number of cheeses at a time, hence its advantage to factories and large cheese-makers.

THE "HOOPS."

What old cheese-makers of twenty years ago called the "cheese-vat" we now call the "hoops." The cheese is pressed on the "hoops" and the "hoops" are greatly superior to the old style of vat. Where farmers, however, have got the old wooden vats these will do right enough for making cheese for home consumption.

SHIPPING SEASON FOR CHEESE.

The manufacture of cheese for export to England will require to begin every year about the middle of November, or early in December, according to the conditions of the season, prices for butter, &c. January and February are the months when the output of cheese will be at its highest. As Cheddar cheese can be shipped when it is a month old the shipping season will thus commence from about the middle of December to first week in January, and continue until about the middle of April. This will land our first manufacture of the season in London about from the middle to the end of January, and the last shipment for the season should reach London on about from the first to the middle of May.

SILOS AND ENSILAGE.

On this subject we have taken numerous extracts from a pamphlet on silos, by J. L. Thompson, late Principal of Dookie College.

The silo system cannot be said to be of recent origin, for we read of the ancient Romans preserving fruits, grains, and forage in a green state in large subterranean vaults. The Mexicans also have practised the same process for centuries, and still preserve a large bulk of their fodder in this way.

The attention of the English-speaking world was first drawn to this subject by the translation by a Mr. Brown (an American) of a work written by a Mr. Augustus Goffart, a distinguished member of the Central Agricultural Society of France. This work was published in New York in 1879, when the subject was quickly taken up by the American people, who have since done much to popularize the system, and there are now in that country thousands of silos.

In 1882 a conference was held at New York of several hundred farmers, who met to compare their various experiences, and the answers to some of the questions considered are very remarkable. Regarding the profitableness of ensilage—

Farmer No. 6 said: "It will double the stock-carrying capacity of our farm; its advantages to dairymen are incalculable."

No. 7 said: "It gives a vigour and healthy appearance not seen in hay-fed cattle. We can double the stock, and thus increase the fertility and value of farms."

No. 8: "It enables one with a little land to keep a large amount of stock."

No. 9: "We believe stock can be kept for one-half the cost of other food, and will fatten as much as during the best grass season."

No. 10: "Anything of vegetable nature that animals will eat will make useful ensilage."

No. 11: "40 or 50 tons of fodder can be ensilaged off one acre, which is worth more than 20 tons of hay."

No. 19: "The cost of feeding on ensilage as against hay and roots is one to three."

No. 20: "I think cattle can be kept for one-fourth the expense of any other method."

No. 28: "One acre of ensilage will keep eight head of cattle 100 days."

No. 30: "I am keeping four times the number of stock with my silos that I have been able to do hitherto. A silo filled with green fodder in time of protracted drought is invaluable."

No. 37: "The profits are very large. I consider my two silos worth £2,000, and would rather pay interest on that amount than give them up."

No. 38: "Ensilage I believe to be the dairyman's anchor on the expensive land of the East. I would as soon think of doing without my house as without a silo. I farm for profits, not for pleasure, and have found the silo the best investment I ever made."

It is needless to multiply these extracts. They are from practical men, whose opinions can be relied upon, and if ensilage is so valuable in America it must be doubly so in these colonies, subject as they are to long periods of drought. It is really astounding that so little has been done to popularize the silos in Victoria. Some years ago the subject was taken up by the Royal Commission on Vegetable Products, and much valuable information was distributed.

Before giving some details concerning the introduction of the silo into these colonies, it may be mentioned that there are now a very great many in England, Scotland, and Ireland, and hundreds of new ones are being built every year. The Messrs. Trepplin, near Kenilworth, Warwickshire, preserve over 5,000 tons every year, and at the Smithfield Club Cattle Show, Islington, 1884, there were 254 exhibits entered for competition, comprising almost every description of plant that could be placed in a silo.

AUSTRALIAN SILOS.

To Mr. Charles Rake, of Olive Farm, Enfield, South Australia, is the credit of introducing the silo into these colonies. Mr. Rake has for a long time been in the habit of taking in all the best agricultural papers in the world, and, observing the apparent success of the silo in America, was not slow to imitate the example. As early as 1880 Mr. Rake built his first silo, and the whole neighbourhood thought he was doomed to disappointment when they saw him putting in tons of succulent green fodder into a pit. Mr. Rake invited his neighbours to come and see the opening of the silo six months afterwards, and, to the surprise of all, found the fodder coming out in excellent condition. Mr. Rake the following year increased his silo capacity to six in number. By this means he was able to produce first-class cream and butter all the year round.

Mr. J. L. Thompson, who was managing "Beefacres," the adjoining estate, at that time, on seeing the success of Mr. Rake's silos, was induced to imitate his example, and in 1884 he built a silo of concrete, which for strength, durability, and convenience, will compare favorably with any silo in the world. This silo consists of four compartments, each 20 feet long, 12 feet wide, and 15 feet deep, having a total capacity of 14,000 cubic feet, and capable of holding 300 tons of green fodder. The cost was about £300, and the structure will last 60 years, bar accident. A sample of ensilage from the first filling of this silo obtained a prize of £10 10s., presented by the proprietors of the *Australasian,* at the National Show, Melbourne, 1885.

When carrying on dairying at the well-known Spring Bank dairy farm near Egerton, Mr. Wilson used to incur heavy losses every summer, owing to the sudden shrinkage in the quantity of milk when the grass dried up. Ensilage being recommended as a summer fodder, he had a silo constructed and filled with chaffed green oats, peas, and maize. The oats and peas were cut and put into the silo in the month of November, and from the same land a crop of maize was ready for the silo by the following April or May. Thus two crops a year were had from the same land, giving an average yield, in the green state, of about 20 tons per acre. The ensilage always turned out well, and lessened the dread of dry summers, scarcity of summer feed, and shortage of milk.

Further practical proof of the value of ensilage for milk-producing purposes, when other feed was scarce, was given at the grounds attached to Government House, Melbourne. Shortly after the arrival in Victoria of Lord Hopetoun, Mr. Wilson, by desire, superintended the cultivation of $3\frac{1}{2}$ acres of poor land at Government House for the growth of two crops a year on it for conversion into ensilage for feed for the Governor's cows during the summer months. This also was a great success, for by applying 30 loads of stable manure per acre to the land a crop of twelve tons per acre of oats and vetches was obtained, followed in the autumn by a twelve-ton crop of maize. This fodder, grown on $3\frac{1}{2}$ acres of land, kept twelve cows in splendid condition right through the whole of the dry weather each summer. The milk and cream produced by the cows fed on the ensilage were pronounced by Lord Hopetoun to be equally as good as when the cows were fed on the spring pastures. These facts have been repeated to farmers in almost every part of Victoria, yet, strange to say, not one in a thousand has yet adopted the system.

CONSTRUCTION OF A SILO.

Local circumstances must determine what material can be most economically used for the construction of a silo. Where plenty of gravel and sharp river sand can be procured nothing in our opinion can equal concrete walls. The division walls should be 2 feet thick, but 18 inches will be sufficient for the outside walls, as these will be built against the excavated bank. One-third of the silo should be above ground and two-thirds below. Doorways as far down as the natural surface should be provided, so as to facilitate the filling of the silo and also the getting out of the ensilage. These openings can be closed up with planks as the silo is being filled, and removed as the ensilage is being taken out. The walls of the silo should be as smooth and plumb as possible, so as to allow the ensilage and covering planks to go down easily as the mass subsides. The walls and bottom of a silo should be air and water-tight. It was thought and recommended at one time to provide drainage at the bottom of the silo, but this is a fallacy, as no moisture should escape from the silo; and a drain that would carry off water would also allow air to get in, which would do a great amount of damage to the ensilage. It has been said that it makes no difference whether a silo cost £20 or £500, one will preserve ensilage as well as the other, the only thing required is continuous pressure. But you cannot make small silos as effective as large ones, nor can you pack the fodder so well against rough surfaces as against walls that are smooth, consequently there is more waste of fodder with small pits and rough surfaces than with large silos and smooth walls.

Cheap earthen silos (holes simply dug in the ground) are more likely to popularize the system of ensilage among the farming community than expensive masonry, and where the earth is sound this plan may be adopted with perfect success.

FILLING THE SILOS.

Before saying anything on this head, it will be as well to state that there|(are now two recognised varieties of ensilage, viz., sweet and sour ensilage. By the term "sour" it must not be understood that the ensilage is in any way offensive ; it has a pale greenish yellow colour, and a slightly vinous odour. Sweet ensilage, on the other hand, is of a brown colour, and of a sweet luscious odour. Sour ensilage has been found to be most suitable for animals producing milk, and sweet ensilage for fattening stock. When it is desired to produce sour ensilage, the crop may be cut when full grown (but before any of the moisture has escaped), and carted to the silo immediately it is cut, and pressed tightly down. The sooner the silo is filled and the weights applied, the better for sour ensilage. If the crops are of a rough nature, such as barley, vetches, maize, &c., they should be pressed through the chaff-cutter, but the finer English grass does not require chaffing. When filled rapidly and immediately weighted, the temperature will seldom exceed 80 deg. Fahr., and little or no fermentation will take place.

SWEET ENSILAGE.

When it is intended to produce sweet ensilage the crop may also be cut when full grown ; but it must lie a day or two in the field, so that, at the time of being put away in the silo, it contains less than 70 per cent. of moisture. The process of filling should go on slowly, so that the temperature may rise from between 125 and 150 deg. Fahr. Should the temperature not be sufficient either the fodder has been too wet, or the filling and consequent compression has been going on rapidly. When a sufficiently high temperature has been obtained, it should immediately be cooled down to below 90 deg. by applying the pressure, or the ensilage will rapidly spoil. The testing the temperature of the silo is a very simple matter. Procure a 12½ feet length} of common inch gas pipe, to this weld a steel point, drive this into the ensilage mass about the centre, and by means of a small glass thermometer and a piece of string you can test the temperature at various depths. I should mention that it is well to put a little wool in the bottom of the pipe to save the glass thermometer in its descent.

COVERING AND CLOSING THE SILO.

The filling of the silo should be carried out in such a manner that the layer of fodder should always be horizontal. The filling having been completed, the covering up takes place. The planks should be put across the short way of the silo, and 9 x 2 redgum is found to be a convenient size. At one time it was thought to be necessary to have the covering as close and air-tight as possible, but this has proved to be a fallacy. Sawdust, bran, felt, boards tongued and grooved, have all been tried in order to prevent the air from escaping ; but the object now is to facilitate the air to escape by compression, and for this purpose it is better to put the planks about a quarter of an inch apart, and half-an-inch shorter at each end than the silo, so that there will be no fear of them sticking against the walls.

WEIGHTING THE SILO.

Mr. Wilson's first experience in weighting the silo was with bags of sand 2 feet deep ; but this was not a success, as the bags soon rotted. He then got the local blacksmith at Egerton, Mr. Simpson, to make a screw and chain press. The screw is worked by one man, and the total leverage of the appliance is as 450 is to 1, due allowance being made for friction. This appliance is a great saving of labour, especially when a silo is being refilled, as the whole covering can be removed in fifteen minutes. In the absence of any mechanical pressure, the weighting can be accomplished by the material easiest procurable on the ground, and that will give sufficient pressure, viz., 100 to 150 lbs. to the square foot. Ensilage can be made in a silo without pressure ; but, taking into account the waste of space and loss of ensilage by decay at the top and sides, this system has no advantage to recommend it. As good ensilage has been preserved in this way as in the most expensive silo, and a small farmer need not hesitate to sink a hole in any good ground, put in his green fodder, and cover it up with 2 feet of earth, and it will come out green and sweet six or nine months afterwards. Wooden portable silos are now much used in England. They are in shape like a huge barrel, and answer the purpose very well in that country; but I doubt very much whether they would be successful in these colonies owing to the excessive heat of our summers. A great deal has been done in England in the way of converting old barns and other buildings into silos.

Opening the Silo.

Only a sufficient number of planks should be removed as to give convenient room for the operation of cutting to be performed. It is best to cut ensilage in vertical sections as is done in a hay-stack, as much being taken out each day as is required for the day's consumption, although it will keep fairly well for a week or so after being removed from the silo. The weights should not be removed from the uncut portions until absolutely required, as it is necessary to continue the pressure as long as possible. When the first cut gets below the surface use a large coal-basket capable of holding 100 lbs. This is raised by means of block and tackle sufficiently high for the man in the dray to catch and empty it. When the silo is small and deep and the consumption rapid, the whole of the weights and coverings may be removed at once, and the ensilage removed from the entire surface as required. In a broad and shallow silo, however, it would be unwise to attempt this method. Ensilage has been taken from a silo of this kind every day except Sunday for three months, and the last was as good as the first.

Crops for the Silo.

Any vegetation that stock will eat in its natural state will make good ensilage, and it will be much improved by the operation, especially if fed to cattle. It is said that cattle assimilate ensilage better than they do any other food, and the reason for this is the change effected in the silo is nearly or quite that which is brought about in the first stomach of the ruminant animal. Barley and tares sown immediately after the first rains are very suitable and profitable for a first filling. These will be ready to put away in the silo, say about the 1st of October, and the land can be at once ploughed and sown with maize, which will be fit for pitting about the end of February. As much as 30 tons per acre of fodder has been obtained in this way without irrigation, i.e., from the two crops. This is sufficient per acre to keep a milch cow for twelve months. Indeed, it has often been proved that by thoroughly cultivating and manuring the land ample food can be grown on an acre for a cow by adopting the ensilage system. Cockspurs variegated, and Scotch thistles, if put away in succulent condition, can be taken out six months later in prime condition, and stock will devour them ravenously. In short, the silo has been styled "the farmer's all"; nothing can come amiss to it. Mangold or turnip tops, cabbage leaves, surplus fodder of any kind can be siloed and kept till periods of want.

We have heard of stock-holders in the interior losing in times of drought all their valuable stud bulls, rams, &c., for want of food. There is really no excuse for this state of affairs. Every few years we have seasons of plenty, when thousands of acres of the natural grasses can be mown and siloed for use in the years of famine. Mr. Walter Lamb, of Rooty Hill and Merilong, Liverpool Plains, New South Wales, has proved to his fellow pastoralists what can be done by means of the silo in storing up fodder in good seasons to save his stock from starvation in periods of drought. Mr. Lamb has siloed over 10,000 tons of the native grasses on his estate at Merilong, and is able to keep a full-grown bullock for twelve months in good condition at a cost of 8s. 9d., and a sheep for 1s. 9d. No man has done so much as Mr. Lamb to demonstrate the great boon that may accrue to the pastoralist in these colonies from the use of the silo. His silos were inexpensive, but answer the purpose well. The weighting is done entirely with earth, and he uses no top covering between the ensilage and the earth.

THE CHEMISTRY OF THE SILO.

It is not intended to touch on the scientific aspect of the silo, but this paper would be incomplete without mentioning that eminent scientists have, as a rule all through, thrown cold water on the subject of ensilage. Professor Custance, of the Roseworthy Agricultural College, South Australia, compared the putting of green fodder in a silo to burying a dead dog. Sir John Lawes and Dr. Volcker have often given the English farmers gentle warnings that ensilage was not worthy of their attention. Lately, however, Sir John has conducted a number of valuable experiments as to the feeding value of ensilage, and has proved that 50 lbs. of ensilage was equal to 84 lbs. of good mangolds.

Mr. A. N. Pearson, our Government Agricultural Chemist, published the result of an analysis of some ensilage submitted to him, and states that 2 lbs. of it are equal to 3 lbs. of good hay. This shows ensilage to be of very great value indeed, and scientific men are now forced to admit there is something in ensilage after all, and certainly progressive farmers of the present day cannot ignore it.

STACK ENSILAGE.

Ensilage has been preserved in good condition in England by simply stacking it green without any silo at all. Mr. H. B. Hughes, of Booyoolic Station, South Australia, stacked a large paddock of lucerne right from his mowing machine. Some time after his stack was built, when his lucerne was 6 inches high, Mr. Hughes put a number of bullocks on to the lucerne, but getting a taste of the stack ensilage they preferred it to the prime succulent green feed. This shows that there is something in the system that improves the fodder, as the tastes of cattle are the best tests of its quality. Mr. Hughes now provides large quantities of ensilage to top up his Queensland bullocks before putting them on the market.

The only objection to stack ensilage is that our penetrating hot winds and sun have the effect of spoiling a considerable portion of the fodder around the edges of the stack, and, although the ensilage can be made well in a stack, the loss is sometimes so great that it will repay the farmer to make a silo.

PRACTICAL RESULTS FROM THE USE OF ENSILAGE.

Wonderful results have been reported as to the value of ensilage on dairy and other stock, but as some of these may be looked upon as " American tall talk," the actual experiences may be given of Mr. J. L. Thompson, formerly Principal of the Dookie Agriculture College. Mr. Thompson writes as follows :—

" When I opened the silos at Beefacres in 1884, about the end of January, our dairy cows were not averaging two gallons of milk a day, and it was almost a matter of imposssibility to make any good butter, although we had a very good dairy. A week after we commenced using ensilage the milk increased to two and three quarter gallons daily, and the butter made from this milk had that peculiar yellow tint so well known as characteristic of good butter. Considering the time of year it was also remarkably firm, and the churning was accomplished in half the usual time. In March of that year we had a clearing sale of 127 Clydesdales and 110 shorthorn cattle. They were fed almost exclusively on ensilage for three months before the sale, and it was remarked by all good judges that they never saw stock looking better or healthier. I can further assert that during the whole of the time this large and valuable number of stock were fed on ensilage there was not one single case of sickness the whole time."

Great excitement was caused in South Australia some years ago when nine horses out of 30 being fed on ensilage died suddenly. Of course, every one said it was the ensilage ; and so it was, but it was largely composed of several very poisonous plants which, if eaten in any condition, would have caused death, and, being chopped up, the stock could not avoid eating them, although in the pasture they could be passed by. No evil results from the use of good fodder made into ensilage has ever come under our notice, but, on the contrary, all stock fed on it have shown a most robust and healthy appearance.

"Ensilage in a nutshell," is simply this :—Every farmer in the spring of the year has abundance of green succulent food for all stock. Then is the period of the year when stock will put on condition, and when any quantity of prime butter can be made. By the use of the silo this abundance of succulent food can be carried right through the year. In the parched month of March, when not a green blade of vegetation can be seen in our fields, you can open your silo full of fresh green fodder, and feed it to your cows, which will give milk that will produce butter quite as good as any you are making at the present time, on what is known as the flower of the grass. This proves, beyond a doubt, that it is not so much the heat of our summers that causes the production of that white frothy-looking butter, so often seen during summer, as the uusuitable nature of the food that cows under ordinary circumstances have to eat.

In England the use of silos and ensilage has passed the experimental stage. Two very important reports bearing on ensilage have been issued, a few extracts from which are taken. These are the reports of the Ensilage Commission, and the Judges of the Royal Agricultural Society's Competition. They are dated May, 1886. Be it noted, the evidence is not that of enthusiastic advocates, but the calm deliberations of judicial bodies appointed to consider and determine as to the value or otherwise of the system. Both bodies emphatically declare ensilage a decided success, and both reports are capable of affording encouragement to British farmers. The Ensilage Commission classify the advantages claimed for ensilage under the following heads :—

1. In rendering the farmer independent of the weather in saving his crops.

2. In increasing the productive capabilities of farms.

3. In greater weight of forage saved.

4. In greater available variety and rotation of crops.

5. In increased facility for storing crops. It is suitable for all kinds of stock—dairy stock, breeding stock, store stock, fattening stock, and farm horses.

The Commissioners, in conclusion, state that they have endeavoured to discount all exaggerated estimates, as well as to make allowance for a considerable amount of prejudice and incredulity which they met with, and they add :—"After summing up the mass of evidence which has reached us we can without hesitation affirm that it has been abundantly and conclusively proved to our satisfaction that the system of preserving green fodder crops promises great advantages to the practical farmer, and, if carried out with a reasonable amount of care and efficiency, should not only provide him with the means of insuring himself to a great extent against unfavorable seasons, and of materially improving the quantity and quality of his dairy produce, but should also enable him to increase appreciably the number of live stock that can be profitably kept upon any given acreage, whether of pasture or arable land, and proportionately the amount of manure available to fertilize it."

The report of the Royal Society's Judges is also very interesting and instructive, and is equally favorable to the system under investigation.

The following concise summary of the experience of the judges of the northern division is worthy of production :—

" We are of opinion that the great question of satisfactorily ensiling green crops has received ample confirmation. It has been proved to us incontestably that its success has been manifested in every district. We have seen silos of brick, of stone, and of wood; we have seen old barns and other buildings converted into silos; we have seen them containing 20 tons, and we have inspected others capable of holding 700 tons; we have found silos constructed at a little over £20, and others at £400 ; we have found them filled with all sorts of green crops, and we have found some sour and some sweet, the latter in by far the greater proportion ; we have seen them weighted with bricks, with stones, with slates, with sand, with earth, and also with ingenious mechanical contrivances; we have inspected some chaffed, and in others the fodder spread out and put in whole; in all cases the practice was successful, and in every instance cattle of all descriptions did well on the silage, and in many instances the opinion was conclusive that decidedly more stock could be carried per acre with silage than with hay. In conclusion, we would say that we consider the system of ensiling will probably affect the future of agriculture on strong land, as in most instances, especially in such where it is necessary to obtain winter foods for the stock, a crop of winter-grown tares or trifolium, or other strong-growing green crops, may be sown in the autumn at little expense, and mown and put in the receptacle by the first week in June, and thus do away with the immense expense and great uncertainty of the cultivation and consumption of roots on such land. The report winds up with the following verdict:—The chief advantage of silage-making against haymaking is its comparative independence of the weather, that the fodder is handled while green without any risk of the tender and nutritious leaves being lost on the ground as in haymaking, that the resulting silage is succulent and palatable, and that on purely grazing farms it is now possible to obtain a portion of the grass crop for winter in such a state as to equal the effect of summer-fed grass for the purposes of the dairy."

In conclusion, it may be added that we cannot continue to keep farms in a high state of fertility without stock, and we cannot keep dairy cattle profitably unless we provide feed for them during periods of drought and consequent famine, and the silo will greatly assist us in this direction.

LIST OF BUTTER FACTORIES IN COLONY OF VICTORIA, WITH CREAMERIES ATTACHED TO SAME.

Name of Factory.	Address.	Secretary or Proprietor.	Creameries Attached.
Ararat ...	Ararat ...	...	Buangor Moyston Great Western Crowlands
Avoca ...	Avoca ...	R. Poynter	Elmhurst Natte Yallock Bung Bong
Aringa ...	Port Fairy ...	J. C. Ritchie	
Alberton ...	Alberton ...	c o Melb. Ch. Br. Co., Melbourne	
Alexandra ...	Alexandra-road ...		Acheson Alexandra-road Crystal Creek Fawcett Thornton Upper Thornton
Benalla ...	Benalla ...	T. S. Moore	Goomalibee Upotipotpon White Gate Tatong Mollyullah Glenrowan
Buninyong ...	Buninyong ...	Jno. Porter	Grenville Clarendon Yendon Napoleons Cargarie Coghill's Creek Learmonth Waubra Lexton Evansford
Buln Buln ...	Buln Buln ...	Melb. C. B. Coy.	
Bear's Creek ...	... ...	Melb. C. B. Coy.	
Bena	Bena		
Baddaginnie ...	Baddaginnie ...	A. Shaw ...	Boho
Balmattum ...	Balmattum ...	A. Wakenshaw	
Benn, F. * ...	Mirboo, Gippsland...	F. Benn	
Burnt Creek* ...	Locksley	G. Akers	
Benambra ...	Benambra ...	Keogh & Browne	
Broad, Mrs. * ...	Elphinstone		

* Private factories.

Name of Factory.	Address.	Secretary or Proprietor,	Creameries Attached.
Broadford	High-street, Broadford	J. T. Brown	Sugarloaf, Glenrona, Northwood, Bailiestown
Beaufort	Beaufort	J. W. Brown	Middle Creek, Stockyard Hill
Bonnie Doon	Bonnie Doon	S. D. Morrissey	Nillahcootie, Howe's Creek, Heyfield
Bolding, Geo.*	Morwell	G. Bolding	
Buckrabanyule	c/o Holdensen and Neilson, Melbourne		
Cowarr	Cowarr		
Colac	Murray-street, Colac	C. A. Tulloh	Cororooke, Beeac, Ondit, Warrion, Nelangil, Alvie
Cobden	Cobden	W. Durbridge	Dixie, Scott's Creek, Port Campbell
Crossover	Gormandale	G. Hare	
Clunes	Clunes	T. H. Reynolds	Talbot, Craigie
Cobrico Cheese Factory	Cobrico	— McKinnon	
Clifford's Cheese Factory	Yerang	— Clifford	
Clyde	Clyde	— Ballantyne	
Caniambo and Gowangardie	Caniambo	E Phillips	
Charlmont Water	via Darnum	R. P. Worth	
Carrajung	Carrajung	J. Tanner	
Coleraine	Coleraine	H. G. Hill	Quinbury, Nareen
Caramut	near Mortlake		
Cox, George*	Taminick		
Clifton Park	Bairnsdale	J. D. & W. Hope	
Cudgewa	Cudgewa	J. S. Ferriss	Colac Colac, Thougla, Cudgewa North
Camperdown	Camperdown	J. Miller	Pomborneit
Calignee	Calignee	J. Holcroft	
Caniambo and Tamleugh	Tamleugh, North Lorne Bay	R. W. Thomas	
Crimeen, B.*	Elphinstone		
Coola	Glenoweith, Euroa		
Clonburn	Katamatite		
Devonshire	Healesville	J. Batchelor	
Drik Drik	Drik Drik	R. A. Lightbody	

* Private factories.

Name of Factory.	Address.	Secretary or Proprietor.	Creameries Attached.
Delatite ...	near Mansfield ...	H. Ricketson	
Daylesford ...	Daylesford ...	W. T. Edwards	Guildford, Glenlyon, Franklingford, Eastern Hill
Diaper's Creek...	... ...	M. C. B. Coy.	
Doubleday, D.*	Bethanga-road		
Dumbalk ...	Meeniyan ...	Findlay ..	Mardan
Devenish ...	Devenish	J. Smallwood	
Dole, J.* ...	Elphinstone		
Doomburrim ...	Fish Creek		
Euroa ...	Euroa	S. Howell	Gooram Gong, Miepoll South, Molka, Creighton Crk., Ragg's Creek, Shean's Creek
Elvezia ...	Yandoit	J. Righetti	
Eskdale ...	Eskdale	J. A. Hailes ...	Tallandoon
Emu	Winton	Chas. Milgaard	
Erinvale* ...	Maindample ...	A. F. Crockett	
Ensay ...	Ensay	J. T. Greenwood	Orbost, Inges
Fletcher, G. H.*	Shepparton ...	G. H. Fletcher	
Farnham ...	Warrnambool ...	A. H. Rennick	Mailor's Flat
Framlingham and Ellerslie	Framlingham, near Warrnambool	L. Durant	Panmure, Purnim, Ballangeich
Fresh Food Co.	Bourke-street, Melbourne	D. Taylor	†

† *Creameries:—*

Newry	Drumanure	Nanneella
Mysia	Towaninny	Timmering
Borung	Pompapiel	Valencia Creek
Wahring	Teddywaddy	Benjeroop
Muskerry	Campbell's Forest	Byrneside
Briagolong	Yarroweyah	Murchison
Salisbury West	Koo-wee-rup	Lake Elizabeth
Bridgewater Nth.	Beazley's Bridge	Moe
Narracan	Budgerum	Quambatook
Glenmaggie	Moorilim	Elmore
Yando	Fernihurst	Bridgewater
Barnedown	Murphy's Lake	Lake Marmal
Sale	Langwornor	Corack East
Redesdale	Nagambie	Yarragon
Tabilk	Mangalore	Powlett Plains
Warrion	Sutton Grange	Girgarre East
Korong Vale	The Heart	Narrewillock
Garvoc	Wunghnu	Coonooer Bridge
Fish Point	Emu Flat	Mystic Park

* Private factories.

Name of Factory.	Address.	Secretary or Proprietor.	Creameries Attached.
Fresh Food Co.	Bourke-street, Melbourne	D. Taylor ...	†

† *Creameries*—continued.

Name of Factory.	Address.	Secretary or Proprietor.	Creameries Attached.
	Lake Charm	Katunga	Glenloth
	Gilgilia	Swan Hill	Wycheproof
	Morwell	Gower East	Koyuga
	Glen Hope	Yeungroon	Kyneton-road
	Tatura	Longwood	Boort
	Terang	Nulla Nulla	Willow Grove
	Richmond Plains		
Geelong ...	Moorabool-street, Geelong	G. Forbes	Ceres Inverleigh Moorabool North Morice Lara Dean's Marsh Murroon Birregurra
Glen Elgin ...	near Barnawatha		
Goulburn Valley	Flinders-lane, Melbourne	— Ballantyne	
Garvoc ...	Panmure	J. R. Vickers ...	Cudgee
Glenelg and Wannon	Casterton ...	F. D'Amaral	
Grasmere ...	Warrnambool ...	I. Williams	Wangoom Cooramook
Glengarry ...	Glengarry ...	J. Bermingham	
Goorambat ...	Goorambat ...	W. Johnston	Stewarton Minuwah
Glenormiston ...	Glenormiston ...	J. Benson	
Goodwin's* ...	Toongabbie ...	S. Goodwin	
Hansen ...	Greta	M. Byrne	Greta West Greta South Moyhu
Hamilton ...	Hamilton... ...	C. H. Smith	Byaduk Croxton Condah Penshurst Victoria Valley
Horsham ...	Horsham	C. E. Lagh	Bungalally Polkemmett Evin's Vale Kalkee Fine View, Jung Jung Vectis East Norton Creek Green Lake Murtoa Black Heath

* Private factory.

Name of Factory.	Address.	Secretary or Proprietor.	Creameries Attached.
Heyfield ...	Heyfield	E. Pallardyce ...	Tinambra
Harvie, A.* ...	Warragul ...	A. Harvie	
Harriss, A. W.*	Warragul ...	A. W. Harriss	
Holdensen and Neilson	Flinders-street, Melbourne	} ...	Irrewillipe Bunbartha Drouin Congupna Rochester Yabba Labertouch Millow Gowangardie Spring Vale
Hazelwood ...	Traralgon		
Jancourt ...	Camperdown ...	D. Mitchell	
Jeeraling ...	Traralgon		
Jilpanger* ...	Gorcke	— Forrests	
Jackson* ...	Euroa	— Jackson	
Kerang ...	Kerang	M. C. B. Coy.	
Kialla ...	Kialla	M. C. B. Coy.	
Kilmore ...	Kilmore	C. J. Osborne	High Camp Plain Wallan Moranding Tallarook
Koroit ...	Koroit	R. Laffan	Woolsthorpe Southern Cross
Koonda ...	Gowangardie East...	J. W. Wilkins	
Kiewa ...	Kiewa Valley, Huon Lane	Rt. Reid ...	3 creameries
Kyneton ...	Kyneton	W. Rogers	Barfold Carlsruhe Drummond Malmsbury Metcalfe Newham Tylden Campbelltown Glendonald Smeaton Kooroochang Ullima
Kilfeera* ...	Benalla	H. Kennedy	
Kongwak ...	near Jumbunna		
Lindenow Cheese Factory	Lindenow ...	M. C. B. Coy.	
Lancefield ...	Lancefield ...	J. Cameron	Rochford Springfield High Camp Plain Baynton

Name of Factory.	Address.	Secretary or Proprietor.	Creameries Attached.
Lang Lang	Lang Lang		
Lillimur	Lillimur	S. Staniland	
Leongatha	Leongatha		
Lake Purrumbete	Weerite	J. J. Quinlan	
Melbourne Chilled Butter	Flinders-lane, Melbourne		†

† Creameries:—

Ardmona	Invergordon	Kaarimba
Cosgrove	Johnsonville	Knowsley
Hillside	Katunga East	Muckatah
Marunga	Naringaningalook	Seven Creeks
Stratford	Undera	Wangaratta
Wanalta	Woodlands	Wy-Yung
Yarroweyah	Fish Creek	Toongabbie
Lower Tarwin	Nicholson	Toora

Name of Factory.	Address.	Secretary or Proprietor.	Creameries Attached.
Merrimu	Bacchus Marsh ...	Anderson & Co.	Ballan
Merrigum	Merrigum ...	— Colbert	
Mirboo North ...	Mirboo North ...	J. W. Nutley	
Mortlake	Mortlake ...	J. McMeekin ...	Kalora
Macarthur	Macarthur ...	J. E Cowling	
Mincha	Mincha	J. McKay	
Morwell	Morwell	— Jones	{ Hazelwood, Driffield, Maryvale, Eel Hole Creek
Mansfield	Mansfield ...	G. Fitzmaurice	{ Barwite, Borrtite
Maintongoon ...	Maintongoon ...	Jas Forsyth	
Miepoll	Tamleugh ...	E. Gallagher	
Merton	Merton	J. J. Hoare	
Major Creek* ...	Major Creek, Burwood	W. Dunlop ...	Yundool
Milawa	Milawa	E. Stuart	{ Bobinawarrah, Tarrawingee, Everton, Sth. Wangaratta, Laceby, Whorouly
Mt. Richmond*	Portland	S. Jennings	
Mornington	Moorooduc, near Mornington	J. E. Jones ...	Boneo
Minyip	Minyip	J. P. McCubben	{ Laen, Dunmunkle, Kewell East
Moyhu	Wangaratta		
Moyarra	Jumbunna ...	A. W. Elms	
Marshall, Wm.*	Morwell	W. Marshall	
Mintaro	Lancefield Junction	W. Moore	
Mokoan	Glenrowan		

* Private factories.

Name of Factory.	Address.	Secretary or Proprietor.	* Creameries Attached.
Myrniong	Myrniong		
Masfield, Mr.*.	Upper Flynn's Creek	Mr. Masfield	
Maher, T.*	Shepparton	T. Maher	
Macorna	c/o Melbourne Chilled Butter, Melbourne		
Mirboo North	Mirboo North		
Nhill	Nhill	J.C.McDonnell	Haycroft Boyeo Woorak Woorak West
Natimuk	Natimuk		
Northwood	Seymour		
Neerim South	Neerim South	F. Beamish	
Oxley	Oxley	J. C. Shanks	
Orbost	Orbost	J. F. Blacklock	
Omeo	Lake Omeo		
Pine Lodge	Pine Lodge		
Pine Grove	Pine Lodge		
Princetown Cheese Fctry.	Princetown		
Poowong	Poowong	E. Dixon	
Portland	Portland	S. P. Hawkins	
Pimpinio	Pimpinio	A. J. Athorn	
Pyramid Hill	Pyramid Hill	A. J. Barnett	
Powlett River	Stony Point		
Pines	Glenrowan		
Ruby	Ruby	Country Creamery Coy.	
Romsey	Romsey	W. H. Snow and Co.	
Rosebrook	Port Fairy	J. C. McCallum	Crossley Kirkstall
River View	Wahring	G. Wicking	
Rosedale	Rosedale	— Wallen	
Rialto Dairy	Flinders-lane, Melbourne	S. V. Meadows	
Swanpool and Moorngag	Moorngag	T. Harrison	
Sale	Sale	E. S. Gutteridge	
Sth. Purrumbete	South Purrumbete	R. Cole	
South Ecklin	South Ecklin	W. Vickers	
Springhurst	Springhurst, Ovens and Murray	H. O. Mardling	Boorhaman Boorhaman N. Gooramadda Noorong Wangaratta N.
Strathbogie	Strathbogie, near Euroa	E. C. Marsh	
Strathbogie Nth.	Strathbogie, near Euroa		

* Private factories.

Name of Factory.	Address.	Secretary or Proprietor.	Creameries Attached.
Sth. Wangaratta	Wangaratta	D. Colson	
Stawell	Stawell	J. W. C. Greene	Lubeck Rupanyup Banyena Callawadda Navarre
Shepparton	Shepparton	T. McNaughten	Cobram N. Mooroopna Numurkah Dunbulbalane Tallygaroopna Congupna Hill Pine Lodge Kialla West
Salathiel, M.*	Elphinstone	M. Salathiel	
Sutton Grange	Sutton Grange	Jos. Young	
Terang	Terang	Geo. McKenzie	
Thorpdale South	Thorpdale South	T. H. Reynolds	
Tower Hill	Illowa	A. Kell	
Tallangatta	Tallangatta	W. H. Dorrington	Tallangatta Vly.
Trafalgar	Trafalgar	S. Giblett	Sunny South Narracan
Traralgon	Traralgon	T. H. Row	Traralgon Sth.
Taggerty	Taggerty	J. B. Coombs	
Tamleugh and Karramomus	Tamleugh	E. Gallagher	
Thoona	Thoona	T. Mitchell	Boweya
Tarwin	Tarwin Lower		
Toora	Toora		
Terip Terip	Yarck	Dawson Bros.	
Taminick	Glenrowan		
Tyers*	Traralgon	D. Gallbraith	
Thornton	Thornton	R. Wightman	
Tungamah	Tungamah		
Tatong*	Tatong, viâ Benalla	D. H. Coghill	
Violet Town*	Violet Town	J. Wallace	Earlston
Victoria Creamy.	South Melbourne	J. Noble	†

† *Creameries:—*

Avenel	Muckleford	Keilor
Baringhup West	Myrtleford	Boort East
Bet Bet	Neerim South	Wild Duck
Corop	Newstead	Jindivick
Runnymede	Sandon	Woodstock
Darbonee	St. James	Bolinda
Gre Gre	Tarago	Sunbury
Kotupna	Ulupna	Whittlesea
Leaghur	Waaia	

Name of Factory.	Address.	Secretary or Proprietor.	Creameries Attached.
Wallace and Milbrook	Wallace	G. F. Holden	Dunnstown Millbrook Bolwarrah Pootila

* Private factories.

Name of Factory.	Address.	Secretary or Proprietor.	Creameries Attached.
Werribee Park	Werribee Park ...	G. T. Chirnside	
Warrenbayne ...	Warrenbayne ...	A. Shaw	
Winton ...	Winton	W. Irving ...	North Winton
Warrnambool ...	Allansford ...	T. Beattie	Nirranda Mepunga East Lake Gillier
Willung ...	Willung, via Rosedale	E. McRae	
Waggarandall *	Waggarandall ...	M. Lalor	
Warragamba* ...	Elmore	Fiedler and Appleby	Pine Grove East
Wright, A. F. S.*	Warragul ...	A. F. S. Wright	
Wattle Creek *	Winton	T. McEwan	
Wilby ...	Wilby	F. H. Lovelock	Boomahnoomoonah Boweya Peechelba Lake Rowan
Warracknabeal	Warracknabeal ...	J. Kelsall	Ailsa Areegra Aubra Bangerang Kellalac
Woodstock ...	on Loddon ...	J. T. H. Cocks	
Woodleigh ...	via Lock		
Warragul ...	Warragul ...	W. H. Snow and Co.	
Wodonga ...	Wodonga ...	A. E. Gibson	
Woodstock ...	Traralgon		
Winchelsea ...	Winchelsea ...	W. Caldom	
Wangaratta ...	Wangaratta ...	— Boase	
Wangaratta Sth.	Wangaratta ...	— Colson	
Wycheproof ...	Wycheproof ...		
White, W. G.*	Flinders-lane, Melbourne	W. G. White	
Yea	High-street, Yea ...	R. A. Wall	Homewood Flowerdale Strath Creek Molesworth Glenburn Murrindindi Terip Terip
Yarram ...	Yarram	T. W. Wyatt	Wonwron Devon Cabrossie
Yarrawonga ...	Yarrawonga ...	Wood & Co.	
Yarra Glen ...	Yarra Glen ...	Wood & Co.	

* Private factories.

Name of Factory.	Address.	Secretary or Proprietor.	Creameries Attached.
Yinnar	Yinnar	F. McCoull	Budgeree Boolarra East Mirboo Fairlie Mid Creek Driffield
Yambuk	Port Fairy	A. Kell	Orford Corbrington
Yannathan	Caldermeade	Westring	
Yarck	near Mansfield		

Sundry Creameries:—

Morrison's	Bass	Yabba
Mt. Wallace	Telford	Gowangardie
Toolem	Burramine	Drouin
Boosey	Oven's Bridge	Labertouche
Youanmite	Bundalong	Spring Vale
Bullengarook	Irrewillipe	Congupna
Oaklands	Rochester	Gheringhap
Boorhamin	Millow	Seymour
North Boorhamin	Bunbartha	Sefton's

By Authority : ROBT. S. BRAIN, Government Printer, Melbourne.

www.ingramcontent.com/pod-product-compliance
Lightning Source LLC
Chambersburg PA
CBHW021628270326
41931CB00008B/916